Grandparents
ARIZONA STYLE

by Mike Link and Kate Crowley

Adventure Publications, Inc.
Cambridge, Minnesota

Dedication:

With thanks and appreciation to Gary and Patty Mondale, whose help and generosity made this book possible.

Photo credits:

Cover photos courtesy of Mike Link and Kate Crowley.

All photos, except page 106, are copyright Mike Link and Kate Crowley.

Cover and book design by Jonathan Norberg

10 9 8 7 6 5 4 3 2 1
Copyright 2010 by Mike Link and Kate Crowley
Published by Adventure Publications, Inc.
820 Cleveland St. S
Cambridge, MN 55008
1-800-678-7006
www.adventurepublications.net
All rights reserved
Printed in China
ISBN-13: 978-1-59193-270-3

Contents

Introduction

Grandparents Arizona Style is for today's grandparents who want to spend more time discovering the world with their grandchildren. This book is about opportunities for adults and children to have fun, laugh and share. Of course, Arizona is ripe with more possibilities than we can cover, but this is a place to get started. We decided to write this book because of our experiences with our grandchildren—three boys and a girl. They provide us with a lot of fun, but we also have a responsibility to them. We can use our time together to help them learn and grow as individuals.

In writing this book we've had to stop and think about the knowledge we've gained, how we learned valuable life lessons and how we could pass our wisdom to our grandchildren. With the changing times, we found that several experiences have become endangered—solitude, silence, open space, dark night skies, free time, reading books and home-cooked food.

Consider the following changes:

1. Farms are no longer a part of most children's experiences. In 1900, farmers accounted for forty percent of our census. By 1990, the total fell below two percent.

2. Open space was once a playground. Now it is slated for development. Children are left with only fenced yards and indoor locations.

3. The "out in the country" experience is disappearing. Urban sprawl means an hour's drive from the inner city to any country areas.

4. Tree climbing is more difficult now. There are few open areas of trees for Jacks and Jills to climb magic beanstalks.

5. The chance to be bored—which is an opportunity to be creative—isn't often in the schedule. Children are signed up for every organized activity and training available, eliminating family time and free time.

6. Sports used to be for fun. Now some parents have children choose a sport, then send them to summer camps where winning is what matters.

7. Canning, pickling and baking—all of those wonderful activities that filled the root-cellars and pantries of the past—are less common.

Today's world has seen some bad and dangerous trends. Fast food (and obesity) is the norm. Meth and other deadly drugs flood our cities, our neighborhoods and our schools.

Fortunately, our grandchildren have us. The role of the grandparent can be different than it was when we were kids, and we can adapt, too. Grandparents have many opportunities:

1. Grandparents are living longer than ever before and can influence their grandchildren longer.

2. Parents work long days, filled with busy hours.

3. Grandparents can provide children with quiet times, new experiences and more play.

4. Grandparents can help introduce children to healthy food; we have the time to prepare it and present it.

5. Children may gain from perspectives other than those of their peers and they may benefit from our guidance and insight.

We may be able to involve the extended family in more activities and be part of the new modern family of the twenty-first century.

That's not to say we should take on the role of mother and father. Instead our place is to supplement a child's parents, to help them wherever our help is wanted and needed. Let's use the time we have with our grandchildren to instill in them important values, to teach them about the world around them and to help shape them into better people.

A Word from Mike Link

"Where are you dad?" "We got a late start and have about an hour till we get to you, why?" "Well you better hurry. Your grandson heard Gampa was coming and now we're sitting out on the curb waiting for you to arrive." An hour later we found our greeting party on the curb, on the blanket. Who could ask for a better welcome than that?

That's the love our grandchildren have for us if we are willing to involve ourselves in their lives. Our greatest gift to them is our love and attention; they are the greatest gift we could receive. We watch all four grandchildren grow; Annalise is now past her first birthday so we are starting the cycle over. The twins (age 4), Aren and Ryan, are fighting the loneliness of having their father in Afghanistan and trying to get all the "man attention" they can from grandpa. (Each twin is engaged in the other's life and a defender of "my brother," yet each is separate in more than looks.) Matthew is five and beginning to look like a young boy rather than a little kid. The passion for Thomas the Train is now gone, pirates and "guys"—any little plastic figure of a person—dominate play now. We need to be mentors, guides and trustworthy companions for the children.

The role of the Grandparent is significant, and played an important part in Kate's life, my life, and those of our children. I spent all my "non-school" time living with my grandparents in Rice Lake, Wisconsin, while my father worked evenings and weekends to try to get us out of the poverty that surrounded us. It was not a desertion of responsibility, but rather a sharing. I was born in Rice Lake, where my grandparents would live until their deaths.

My dad worked second shift, from three pm to midnight, and that meant we had little time together, so my grandfather taught me to play catch, to drive, to work. He was my partner. My grandmother picked berries with me, taught me the pleasure of fresh baked pies and cookies. She was the stern partner who could laugh, but I saw her more as the person who ran the home. My second set of grandparents were in the same town and I remember the kolaches that my grandmother made, the canary in the living room, but not much more since they were not the type to play and share warmth with me.

I was also lucky to know my great grandparents and to see my heritage through this multi-level set of grandparents. It was a wonderful way to connect time and generations. My great-great grandmother, Ogima Benisi Kwe (Chief Bird Woman), was from the La Court O'Reilles reservation and she married my great-great grandfather John Quaderer who was from Liechtenstein.

Their daughter, Anna Kahl, my great grandmother, was a wonderful woman who raised not only her 13 children on their farm, but also raised five of my uncles who would move back to the reservation as they reached adulthood. She carried forward the tradition that a grandparent should be the role model and the teacher, while the parents provide safety, home, food and provisions. I will always remember her in her polka dot dress and brimmed hat. She loved her hat and when her daughters threatened to throw it away, she cut off the brim and pretended it was a new hat that, therefore, could not be thrown out. She is part of who I am. My Anishanabe heritage created the succession of grandparent/grandchild roles and bonds that continues today. I believe that the extended role of the traditional grandparent is one that fits the needs of today.

My parents stepped forward to provide support and love for my children and took them traveling, letting them try things that they had to do to learn and grow. Most of all, my children knew they loved them.

Now we have our grandchildren living in two states. Matthew is closest to us, one hundred miles away, and lives where we travel regularly. This gives us the benefit of regular short visits, a few weekends, and a few travel weeks. This is a great mix, one that allows us to jump in, have a great time and leave, but not to spoil him.

We want to support our children and our grandchildren and we take our own admonition "be a companion, not a checkbook, be supportive, not a chauffeur." I cannot tell you what presents my grandparents gave me, but I do know about the things we did together. If you want to build those memories, get going; take those grandchildren and experience the world again for the first time through their curiosity.

We are the elders; we are the starting point for more generations. A Lakota friend told me that growing old does not make you an elder. Be yourself. Be honest, be fun, be open. Grandchildren are gifts from the future—they connect us to their world, and we in turn owe them a connection to ours.

A Word from Kate Crowley

Most of us, if we're lucky, have known our grandparents. We are even luckier if those grandparents lived nearby and enriched our lives. Until the last 50 years, elders have been integral and respected members of our communities. They transported the stories, the history of the people. They were revered and children spent time in their company. The Industrial Revolution, while it has brought us lives of relative ease and abundance, has also brought about the gradual decline of the close-knit, extended family.

Much of the knowledge that the elders, the grandparents, carried was tied to life on the land. Older grandparents, and those of the generation who are just now becoming grandparents, are the last generation where a majority can remember a time when grandparents lived on farms or in small towns. We can recall the easy, simple times spent with these adults who indulged us; we can share memories with a generation being born into a century with untold opportunities and, unfortunately, too many uncertainties.

By the time I was born, I only had two living grandmothers. One lived in California and I have very fuzzy memories of her. My other grandmother lived just a block away from our house and though her Germanic heritage didn't incline her toward a warm, cuddly exterior, I had over 20 years of close acquaintance with her. I even lived with her for four years during and after high school. She was a working woman into her 80s—ironing clothes for people and caring for one or two elderly people in her home, so she didn't have the time or personality to get down on the floor and play with us. But her house was always open to us and we wore a path through our neighbors' backyards to get there. She had a few old toys and books for us to play with and a big old piano, but mostly we came to visit and if we were lucky, on a hot summer day, she'd make us a root beer float.

A Sunday ritual for the first 16 years of my life was dinner at "Ma's," as we called her: roasted chicken, mashed potatoes and gravy, cooked corn, cabbage salad, and either apple or custard pie. I only have to think about it and I'm coming through her front door into a room moist with the steam of cooked vegetables.

Our most firmly held memories of time spent with our grandparents are tied to our senses. These are the things that will stay with children as they grow to adulthood and recall their times spent with their grandparents. That, and laughter.

One of the most mouthwatering memories I have is a summer day picking tomatoes with my grandmother. It was a hot day and the sun was beating down on us as we moved through the pungent rows of tomato plants. I must have been old enough to be considered trustworthy—she expected me to pick the right ones and handle them properly. What do I remember most about that day? That she packed cheese sandwiches (probably Velveeta) and I have never eaten anything more delicious than a rich, sweet tomato right off the vine, still holding the sun's heat, with juice running down my chin, followed up by a bite of soft cheese on white bread. The smells and tastes flowed together and I can still see us, joined together by the simple act of harvesting our food.

I have waited a very long time to become a grandmother and not just because our daughters chose to wait until their 30s to have children. Even when my two children were still pre-teens, I was contemplating grandparenthood. I changed my first name from Kathy to Kate because I couldn't picture a "grandma Kathy." I packed away all the Fisher Price toys in their original boxes to share with the next generation and saved as many of their books as possible. I enjoyed raising my two children and I knew I wanted to have similar experiences again, but without the worries and day-to-day concerns that accompany young parenthood. I knew even then that as a grandparent I would be able to have fun, play with the kids, act silly, share what I've learned in life with them, but have the luxury of going home at the end of the day to a quiet, clean house.

Now we have three grandsons—all arrived in the span of one year, and a granddaughter to counterbalance all that testosterone, and we are looking forward to years of adventures together. Matthew, Ryan, Aren and Annalise are more precious to me than I could've imagined, just as I know your grandchildren are for you. We are not reliving our childhood through them, as some might think, we are participating in their journey into the future—a future we can only imagine. And we want our journey together to be as much fun and full of learning and discovery as possible. This is why we have written this book—this Field Guide—to help other grandparents find those unique and unforgettable places that will combine fun and facts, history and humor, excitement and enduring memories for you and the special children in your lives.

How to Use This Book

The suggestions in this book are just suggestions. Some experiences are unmatchable anywhere else in the state. Others can be replicated. If you are not near the museum, park or site we highlight, find a similar place near you. Read our suggestions and pay special attention to "Bonding and bridging" to tie your visit to a life lesson.

We do not advocate that you become the "wallet" or the "chauffeur." Consider an active participation in friendship and sharing that is enriched by love. We want you to receive the respect due an elder, to share your experience and to enjoy the love that can flow between generations.

One of the themes of this book is that things change. This is true for everything, including the state's attractions. They sometimes close, renovate or move. When in doubt, *CALL BEFORE YOU LEAVE HOME.*

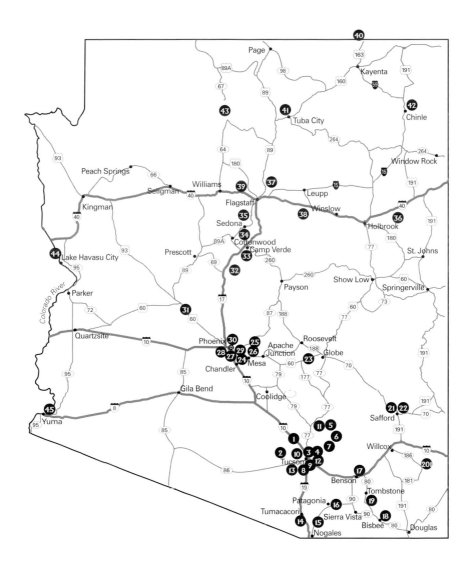

Page
163
40
98
Kayenta
191
89A
160
59
67
89
43
41
42
Tuba City
Chinle
64
264
89
Window Rock
180
93
264
Peach Springs
66
15
191
Williams
39
37
Seligman
Leupp
40
Flagstaff
38
Winslow
36
Kingman
35
40
Sedona
191
Holbrook
40
34
180
89A
Cottonwood
St. Johns
Camp Verde
33
77
Prescott
69
260
44
Lake Havasu City
93
32
95
260
Show Low
60
Springerville
17
Payson
Colorado River
89
73
Parker
60
87
188
72
60
31
Roosevelt
Quartzsite
30
25
188
Globe
191
10
Phoenix
29
26
Apache
28
24
Junction
23
27
Mesa
70
Chandler
60
85
79
177
77
Gila Bend
10
Coolidge
79
77
21
22
8
79
Safford
191
45
85
191
70
Yuma
95
10
Willcox
11
5
86
77
1
6
20
2
10
3
4
7
186
10
Tucson
9
8
12
17
Benson
80
181
13
19
Tombstone
Patagonia
90
19
Tumacacori
16
Sierra Vista
90
18
14
Bisbee
80
15
Nogales
Douglas

The sites appear in the book in the order below, beginning with those in Tucson and the southeastern part of the state, proceeding north and then west.

White Stallion Ranch

We grandparents grew up with Westerns, whether they were the Saturday matinees or Saturday morning TV shows. Roy Rogers and Dale Evans, *Gunsmoke, Bonanza, Sky King, Have Gun—Will Travel*, all of them filled our imaginations with adventure, good guys and bad guys, and horses, always horses. It seems that all kids, even today, go through a "horse" stage. Some of us never really outgrow it.

Arizona still epitomizes the Old West and the cowboy life to many people, but the real west was a harsher world. Violence and the struggle to survive in an unforgiving climate were daily realities, far different from the idealized Old West full of ranches and gunfights.

While gunfights weren't as prevalent in the west as the movies suggest, ranches were a big part of the settlement of Arizona and in the twentieth century, folks out east decided they'd like to have a civilized taste of that era and Dude Ranches were born. In the 1940s there were 100 guest ranches in the Tucson area alone, but today urban sprawl and the rising cost of liability insurance have pushed most out of existence.

The White Stallion Ranch is only one of two remaining guest ranches in Tucson. Originally built in the 1900s as a working cattle ranch, it changed hands four times in the twentieth century. The True family bought it in 1965 and today Russell and Michael, second-generation Trues, continue to operate the ranch. They have brought it into the twenty-first century by accommodating the recreational interests of today's visitor. The ranch covers 3,000 acres and is bordered by the Saguaro National Park and the Tucson Mountains. It has been the location for numerous commercials and TV productions—most notably scenes from *High Chaparral*—and it still has over 125 cattle, which are part of the experience too.

Those who grew up in urban areas may have had access to riding stables or relatives in the country with horses. Our grandchildren have far fewer opportunities to experience this; a Dude Ranch vacation is a very special way to introduce grandkids to horses and some of the romance of the old Westerns. Of all the activities we recommend, it is the most expensive, but if you have the means and a grandchild who really loves horses, then sharing a few days at a Dude Ranch could be the best time you spend together.

Bonding and bridging:

Animals are one of the best forms of therapy in the world. We can tell them our secrets and frustrations and dreams and they just listen. We can lavish attention on them, groom them, pet them and not need anything in return. At a Dude Ranch you and your grandchild may each be assigned one horse to use during your stay (your grandchild may prefer this) and it will become "their" horse during this vacation. This is a good time to share with them stories of pets you had as a child and how special they were to you, how they helped you through difficult times. Learning to care for another living being, whether big or small, is an important life experience for your grandchild. If you are unable to take your grandchild to a Dude Ranch, consider a visit to a riding stable, where you can still share the experience of exploring the countryside on horseback, with a cowboy or cowgirl as a guide.

A word to the wise:

Horses are large and powerful animals, and there is always a risk involved when we spend time on or around them. Cowboy hats are fine for wearing around the ranch, but when going out for a ride, make sure the kids are wearing riding helmets. Some ranches provide them, but others may not, so be prepared to bring your own. Talk to the children often about the need to exercise caution around horses and follow the wranglers' rules and instructions at all times.

Age of grandchild: 9 and older

Best season: Fall–spring

Contact: White Stallion Ranch, 9251 W Twin Peaks Road, Tucson, AZ 85743 • Phone Number: (520) 297-0252; (888) 977-2624 • www.wsranch.com

Also check out:

MacDonald's Ranch: www.macdonaldsranch.com

Triangle T Guest Ranch: www.triangletguestranch.com

Mountain Ranch Stables: www.mountainranchresort.com

Rocking K Ranch Stables: (520) 647-0040

Old Tucson Studios

Was that John Wayne walking down the dusty road or James Stewart, or Dean Martin, or Ricky Nelson or Walter Brennan? This wasn't the real West, but it was the West that Hollywood created to woo Grandpa and Grandma to the romance of the Old West. Take the tour if you want to know what movie

was shot in specific locations and to get a sense of how important this area has been in western movie lore, but remember that your grandchild won't know these movies, so think about their interest level before taking them on the walk.

The town and all the old buildings are intriguing by themselves and you can talk about the movies and TV shows you have seen that were filmed here and compare that with what they might have seen in a real village in the Old West.

The best way for kids to get into the mystique of the setting is to ride the train that loops around the set and the stage coach that gives you a ride through the town and out to the other sets. These are fun and add to the adventure because they make you feel like you are participating in one of the stories. There are also horseback rides and a merry-go-round for young children. Let them enjoy the added memories of these simple rides.

The dramas played out on the streets and in the saloons are the most entertaining aspect of Old Tucson. Real actors exchange gunshots, tumble from roofs, and exchange menacing looks in small vignettes of western lore. Afterward, the cowboys that have been shot (and those who shot them) rise from the dust and visit with the tourists, exchanging handshakes, posing for photos, and teasing the young buckaroos. In the saloon you can sing along with the dancehall girls and enjoy the spectacle of this localized musical. You might want to eat some barbeque here, get a little firewater in the saloon (alcoholic or non-alcoholic), and sit and watch clips of the old westerns that were filmed here.

Old Tucson has many other ways to enjoy your visit, including trail rides, gold panning, and shooting galleries, so give yourself time to enjoy them all. Remember this is a commercial operation so there are charges for these activities and you need to keep in mind how much you are willing to spend for a day with the Duke, Roy, Gene or Hoppy!

Bonding and bridging:

Mike has acquired DVDs of the old black-and-white television westerns he loved as a child, and today his grandsons sit on his lap and watch them with the same enthusiasm, as they both root for the good guys with grandpa. The Old Tucson Studios website includes a list of movies shot on site so you can make plans for a pre- and post-trip movie experience. This is fun as a trip down memory lane, but think about it as a way of sharing perspective with your grandchild, which will allow them to differentiate between the (relative) truth of history from the fantasy of entertainment. The stories of the Old West are told over and over in film and print, but they are always different. How can this be? It is important for them to know that movies and western books are made to do two things—make money and entertain, not to convey facts. Other types of books (such as textbooks) contain facts, and we can help them to learn the difference.

A word to the wise:

Old Tucson Studios is surrounded by the Tucson Mountains; a large portion of the mountains fall within a park owned by the city. Without this natural setting, the site would not be as valuable. While our cities and urban landscapes change rapidly, the natural world sets a slow pace and it is the setting of cactus and raw mountain peaks that help give the location a timelessness.

Age of grandchild: 5 and up

Best season: Avoid the midday heat in summer

Contact: 201 S Kinney Road, Tucson, AZ 85735 • (520) 883-0100 • www.oldtucson.com

Also check out:

Oatman: http://oatmangoldroad.org

City of Tombstone: www.cityoftombstone.com

Rawhide Western Town and Steakhouse: www.rawhide.com

Goldfield Ghost Town: www.goldfieldghosttown.com

Gammons Gulch: www.gammonsgulch.com

Rex Allen Museum: www.rexallenmuseum.org

All Souls Procession

The sky is dark, the crowd is building. Musicians play strange percussive objects that look like they come from your home plumbing. A car is decorated with a hundred candles by a woman in fishnet stockings, brilliant

colors and exotic makeup. Trains rumble by on the track nearby, seemingly part of the tableau, but in fact they are just following their normal schedule. Large balloons are lit by spotlights and a screen stands above the crowd showing faces and memories of passed loved ones. Then people move in, some with faces painted to look like skeletons and others in costumes of the dead and the near dead.

But no one is afraid; in fact, people are smiling, laughing, ready for a celebration. It is the All Souls Procession in Tucson and there is nothing else like it. It is a night of parades and something like a southwestern version of Mardi Gras, except it is held as a celebration that takes the sting of death and turns it inside out. You can choose to be at the University for the beginning or you can be at the grand finale stage, the site we have described here.

This is an activity to save for grandchildren that are old enough to recognize that people dressed like the dead are just actors in this annual live theater production. The events take place after dark, and will last until ten o'clock or later—another reason to bring the pre-teen or teenager. This is a community event that has grown larger each year and there is a sense of camaraderie and respect between all who join in. The weird costumes and sounds and sights are all around you. How will you explain this? First of all, have fun. Laugh, share the images you see; let them explore the fascination that comes with the light and the dark and the strange characters, and perhaps you can take out some of the fear of night, if not death.

If you are in costume, you can join the parade route with the others, but no matter what you do, stay for the grand finale. There you'll find dance, rhythm and costumes; acrobats performing in the air, light shows and sparklers; all combined into a dazzling display of play and movement. Once the performance begins, the kids will have so much to see that is unique that the waiting will be worth it.

Bonding and bridging:

Think about the idea of staying up late, of being out after dark! We know that being out after dark is not a big deal to grandparents who'd rather be in a warm, cozy bed instead of being outside in a crowd, but that would deny both you and your grandchild one of the most memorable visual and auditory experiences you will ever have. This is an adventure and there is a feeling of safety being with their grandparents. For teens, it is likely to up your "cool" quotient significantly. You can be a guide for them or let them guide you. Is this art? Is it drama? Talk about what this represents to both of you. You can also talk about Halloween and where it comes from. Why do people dress in costume? Halloween is based on All Souls' Day, on the Day of the Dead, a traditional form of celebration in Mexico. It is about learning to accept death as part of our lives and we can laugh at the demons of our imagination. 500 years ago, the Spaniards saw a performance that was similar to what you are encountering and, like now, the people were laughing at death.

A word to the wise:

As the parade makes its way to the stage area, the crowd gets packed close together. Anyone less than five feet tall will have to be held or you need to stake out a spot up near the stages. This means coming early and waiting until all the parade participants have arrived. This can mean lots of standing and lots of waiting. Make sure you have some snacks, but remember that getting to a bathroom can be a challenge, so limit the amount of liquids. It is a good place to bring the handheld games kids like or to have things that can be played with while standing in place. You want the kids to be entertained or you will suffer. But also, be aware that the crowd becomes so large prior to performance that you will not have much room. Plan ahead!!!

Age of grandchild: 10 and up

Best season: October and November around Halloween

Contact: All Souls Procession: www.allsoulsprocession.org

Also check out:

Day of the Dead: www.azcentral.com/ent/dead/articles/dead-history.html

Day of the Dead in Mexico: www.dayofthedead.com

Tucson events: www.visittucson.org

It is not a slight thing when they who are so fresh from God, love us. CHARLES DICKENS

Postal History Foundation

Have you ever wondered where or when the first stamp was produced? The answer is 1840 in England. This was the first adhesive stamp. Beginning in 1661, letters were hand stamped or postmarked in ink. This and many more interesting facts can be found at the Postal History Foundation in Tucson. It is also where you and your grandchildren can go to learn about philately (pronounced fil-aht-el-ly)—the hobby of stamp collecting. This is an activity that has gotten the same sort of negative stereotype as bird-watching—both are considered somewhat nerdy. In some ways the two hobbies are similar, since they're about seeing unique and often beautiful creations, though the postage stamps are manmade. In the days before computer games and Wii and other electronic distractions, many kids collected stamps. It was a cheap and easy hobby. But like many other childhood hobbies, it fades in the teen years and returns in later adulthood. The 50 volunteers and three staff who operate the Postal History Foundation in Tucson are some of those folks. In a small building near the University of Arizona campus they share their love of stamps—and inform you about the variety of stamps, postal history, and the stories behind them.

Inside there is an 1890s Post Office from Naco, with a variety of old equipment that will fascinate young and old. The main room is for processing the stamps that arrive by the thousands. Volunteers sit at tables and laboriously sort them into the proper categories for filing. Another room has changing exhibits related to stamps and their history and third room is set up so that kids of all ages can come to learn and be actively involved in the sorting and cataloging of the stamps (more than 8,500 children visit annually). The volunteers who will give you a tour want to share their enthusiasm for this lifelong hobby and it's very likely they will find a special worksheet that combines stamps and various topics (butterflies, birds, ocean life, etc.) for your grandchild to take home. This is a working Post Office too, so if you would like to mail something, you can do so here. Also the Slusser Philatelic Library is next door; it is designed mainly for research purposes, but it has a kids' "corner" and a special treasure chest where your grandchild can dig through and find some special souvenir stamps to bring home.

Bonding and bridging:

Do you remember getting your first piece of mail? Did you have a pen pal? How things have changed. Our grandchildren are growing up with bits, tweets and twitters. It is certain they won't be saving their emails to pass along to their descendants, but we can be a part in saving at least a tiny bit of the past. We can start when the children are very young, by sending them postcards when we travel. We know that our four grandchildren run with glee when the mailman delivers a postcard addressed to them. Right now the words don't matter as much as the pictures on the card, or the fact that they got a piece of mail, but as they grow older, the message will mean something too. And when they are traveling with us, we help them write and mail postcards home. As for stamps, you can have fun picking out stamps for the kids and using special ones when you mail cards or letters to them. Even better, today you can make your own postage stamps with your favorite photos. What better way to start a collection?

A word to the wise:

If you have a stamp collection and want to share it with your grandchild, start in small sections and include stories with the various stamps. Too many at one time will overwhelm them and their eyes will glaze over. They will be fascinated at the difference in the price of stamps over time. It's hard to believe that we once paid only three cents for a stamp in our lifetime, and soon it will be nearly half a dollar. But we need to let them know why stamps cost more now (increased transportation and labor costs, decrease in regular mail due to email) and the importance of having a public postal service.

Age of grandchild: 5–early teens

Best season: Any season

Contact: 920 N First Avenue, Tucson, AZ 85719 • (520) 623-6652 • www.postalhistoryfoundation.org

Also check out:

ARIPEX Stamp Show: www.aripexonline.com

Arizona stamp clubs: www.afsconline.com

Historic Kingman Post Office:
http://kingmanhistoricdistrict.com/buildings/kingman-post-office

Forget not that the earth delights to feel your bare feet, and the winds long to play with your hair. Kahlil Gibran

Closer to Nature (and the Stars) on Mount Lemmon

Imagine describing a trip north from Tucson to the pine forests along the Canadian border. You'd probably need a week to cover the variations in climate and vegetation, but if you drive to the top of Mount Lemmon, you can see all this in an afternoon! That's right. Driving to the top of Mount Lemmon is like a trip to the far north without having to pack your bags. As

you go up in elevation, the plants and animals you see will change and this is a great way to learn about ecology, plant communities and the variations in nature. As you drive uphill, there are numerous places for you to pull over and take photographs or just absorb the scenery of the Catalina Mountains. This is also a good place to teach your grandchildren about maps. As you look at the landscape below, spread out a map and see if they can orient themselves with what they see.

There are also hiking options—great places to explore, get exercise, watch birds, and note the vegetation. Check out the trail distances and difficulty in advance if possible. There will be dramatic canyons, as well as plateaus you can walk out on. There are rock hoodoos like those found in the Chiricahua National Monument and each formation has a unique shape. It's fun to come up with names for them (which is much more fun than to read a name someone else gave it). In the summer, walk the pine woods and it feels like you are on the Canadian border.

A night with the stars is a unique way to enjoy the high elevation above the city. Near the summit of the 9,000-foot peak, the University of Arizona's Sky Center invites the public to view the heavens. This requires reservations, but is well worth the effort. The center offers two events, Sky Nights and Discovery Days, which pair you with University professors and students and help you see the details in both the day and the night.

If you are here in the winter, downhill skiing could be your treat. This is the southernmost alpine ski area in the US and it is a wonderful getaway from the desert below. There is a resort with equipment, lifts, and a lodge near the summit, and even a small grocery store. All of this takes place in a portion of Coronado National Forest. The National Forests are wonderful places for recreation and inspiration and this scenic road is truly one of Arizona's gems.

Bonding and bridging:

In 1899, a scientist named C. Hart Merriam published a study that referred to "life zones," which described ranges of habitat. His life zones ranged from the Lower Sonoran (low, hot desert) to the Arctic-Alpine (alpine meadows or tundra) and everything in between. Today the classifications are seen as too simplistic, but for you and your grandchildren it is a fun checklist of what you see as you drive up the mountain. One of the reasons people come up here is to cool off. While the air in Tucson might be hot, the air cools nearly 5 degrees for every 1,000 feet of elevation gain. By the time you near the summit, it might be as much as thirty degrees cooler and you may wish you had brought a jacket along. Be prepared. You must also prepare for snow in the winter months.

A word to the wise:

To truly enjoy the mountain you need to spend most of a day here. (If you are doing astronomy, it might be most of a night.) That means extra planning, meals and maybe even camping gear. You might want to use one of the campsites near the top and expand your experience, or you might just want to have cots or air mattresses for a siesta in the high elevation sun. But remember that the atmosphere in the higher elevations is thinner and sunscreen is important.

Age of grandchild: 6 and up

Best season: All

Contact: Coronado National Forest, 300 W Congress Street, Tucson, AZ 85701 • (520) 388-8300 • www.fs.fed.us/r3/coronado

Palisades Visitor Center, Mile 20, Catalina Hwy • (520) 749-8700

Also check out:

Forest Road 300 on the Mogollon Rim: www.fs.fed.us/r3/coconino/recreation/mog_rim/rim-road-scenic.shtml

Arizona Scenic Roads: www.arizonascenicroads.com

Coronado Trail Scenic Byway: www.fs.fed.us/r3/asnf/recreation/scenic.shtml

Red Rock Scenic Byway: http://redrockscenicbyway.com/

I like to walk with Grandpa, his steps are short like mine. He doesn't say, 'Now hurry up." He always takes his time. Unknown

Snow Fun

Arizona is a land of deserts, no one would downhill ski here—or would they? Two options let you leave the lowlands with their cactus and travel up into the pine and spruce forests and romp in snow and enjoy the pleasure of the slopes. Right above Tucson in the Catalina Mountains is Mount Lemmon— the southernmost ski area in the United States! The other is the Arizona Snowbowl in the San Francisco Peaks above Flagstaff where there is deep white snow and ski runs filled with powder.

There are other places to enjoy winter fun in Arizona. In eastern Arizona, Sunrise Ski Lodge on the Mogollon Ridge provides both downhill and cross-country skiing, and one can go tubing in the White Mountains. Near Williams, Elk Ridge has a family ski, tubing and snowboard recreation area. The operation at Williams includes a tow rope (which can be an adventure in itself.)

In addition to the thrill of downhill skiing, the Nordic Center near Flagstaff allows you to enjoy the quiet beauty of cross-country skiing and snowshoeing. Snowshoeing is the easiest skill to teach grandchildren. It is fun, simple, and takes just a few minutes to learn.

Skiing skills are much more difficult to learn, and you need to have a good instructor to help your grandchild get the most enjoyment. We recommend that you accompany them, but let someone professional give them their lessons. This limits frustrations since most grandparents are not trained instructors and it also means the children get to learn the latest techniques. Ski training for children is available at Snowbowl and is divided by ages and can involve either skis or snowboards. The training is a half day or a full day with instructors who know how to encourage and train your grandchildren so that you can cheer them on and join them as their skills develop.

If skiing is too difficult, sledding is another easy, intuitive option. Nothing is more exhilarating, and sledding is guaranteed to get smiles and laughter and it only requires a minimum of gear. You can sled at the Crowley Pit just one mile past the Nordic center, where tubes, sleds and toboggans are available. Whichever winter activity you choose, imagine telling friends that you embarked upon these winter adventures in Arizona!

Bonding and bridging:

Those of us who grew up in colder climates (and there are many Arizona grandparents that fit that description) remember the fun of sledding and possibly skiing. It seemed that the cold didn't penetrate through our clothing and skin as quickly as it does now. Snow is such a magical substance; kids really can't get enough of it. As long as kids are dressed properly and have the right mindset, any outing, whether sledding, snowshoeing or skiing will be fun. Just make sure to pay attention so your grandchild's hands and feet don't get cold—nothing ruins a winter outing as quickly as painful fingers or toes.

Your visits to the mountains don't have to happen in winter. The ski lifts at both sites are open in the summer months and give you a cool break from the desert climate while allowing you to view the beauty of the landscape for miles in all directions.

A word to the wise:

Mount Lemmon is 9,157 feet tall and the lifts at the Snowbowl in Flagstaff start at 9,500 feet and take you to 11,500 feet, so elevation can be a factor for all skiers. A case of altitude sickness can come on quickly and takes hours to go away. Exertion at these heights can bring it on more quickly. Since this is mountain travel, it also pays to check the road conditions before you go and make sure the roads are safe to travel. For the road to Mount Lemmon call the Pima County Sheriff's 24-hour Road Condition Hotline (520-547-7510).

Age of grandchild: 5 and up

Best season: Winter

Contact: Mount Lemmon Ski Valley: www.fs.fed.us/r3/coronado/forest/recreation/winter_activities/winter.shtml

Also check out:

Arizona Snowbowl: www.arizonasnowbowl.com

Flagstaff cross-country ski center: www.flagstaffnordiccenter.com

Sunrise Park Resort, Greer: www.sunriseskipark.com

Elk Ridge Ski and Outdoor Recreation Area, Williams: www.elkridgeski.com

Sabino Canyon

Early morning in Sabino Canyon brings out much more than birds and grazing animals, it also brings out people come from all corners to exercise while enjoying the natural surroundings and the cool morning weather.

There are those who come by bike, followed by waves of walkers—seniors, young families, grandparents and grandchildren, groups of friends, bird watchers and exercise buffs. (The paved road is closed to bikes Wednesday and Saturday and between 9 am and 5 pm.)

Here saguaros mix with cottonwoods, willows and sycamores in the valley bottom. The slopes are high and dry, while the valley bottom catches the water from the upper slopes and the shade prevents it from evaporating. This same shade allows you and your grandchild to hike in relative comfort. There are nine low bridges that cross the stream as you walk up. Many have small pools with fish in them and your grandchildren can play in the water. But this canyon does have rattlesnakes and sometimes they too like to cool off near water, so use caution. Don't be afraid, just be aware.

There are many things to do along this hike, but be prepared for a stroll that follows an incline. Bring a wagon or a stroller as a backup, but if you and your grandchild are more agile and looking for more adventure, there is an easy trail among the cactus along the first mile and we found ourselves alone, even though there were hundreds of people on the roadway.

This is a recreation area, so there are bathrooms and picnic tables at various points along the trail where you can enjoy treats, relax and let the children play. Older kids are able to enjoy more challenging hikes that branch off and lead up the canyon walls and away from the crowds. Sabino Lake Trail takes you to a wetland bird-watching spot that is especially good in the spring and early summer. Phone Line Trail heads up the south slope and provides spectacular views of the canyon after you have worked your way up.

To make things even more family-friendly, there is a shuttle bus that takes you up and down the roadway, where no cars are allowed. This means you can ride up the canyon and walk down, or you can walk, catch a ride, get off and walk again.

Bonding and bridging:

The visitor center at the entrance is a good place for orientation, although you might want to go there after your hike if you do an early morning walk, since they are not open until 8 am. This is a small place with gift store, limited refreshments, bathrooms and some nice displays about the Canyon that you can use to talk about the walk you just completed or the one you are about to take. The gift store has items that are appropriate for kids of all ages to help reinforce what they saw or experienced.

There is a small nature trail outside the visitor center where you can learn the names of plants as a warm up. You can relax in the shade in front of the visitor center and if you are there early or late you will probably see birds up close. They too like the shade. There may also be some rabbits and lizards to watch!

A word to the wise:

Friends of Sabino Canyon has a full coloring book on their website. You can download the entire book or just a page to color or a puzzle to do. Each activity allows your grandchild to explore another aspect of the canyon. There are plants, birds, mammals, mazes and puzzles in the collection. If you do this with them, they will enjoy your company and you can also talk about the pictures and what they show. This way you can do an interactive nature lesson and you can bring along the pages to see if you can find these items on your walk. You can also go to www.sabinocanyon4kids.com for an excellent site that is focused on kids and the canyon!

Age of grandchild: 5 and up, unless you use a stroller

Best season: Spring, winter and fall to avoid the heat

Contact: Sabino Canyon Visitor Center: 5700 N Sabino Canyon Road, Tucson, AZ 85750 • (520) 749-8700

Sabino Canyon Recreation Area: www.fs.fed.us/r3/coronado/forest/recreation/camping/sites/sabino.shtml

Also check out:

Catalina State Park: http://azstateparks.com/parks/cata

Cave Creek Canyon: www.fs.fed.us/r3/coronado/forest/recreation/scenic_drives/cave_cr.shtml

It's All Happening at the Zoo

Collections of exotic animals have existed at least since the time of the pharaohs. Until the first public zoos were created, zoos were essentially private collections of animals owned by the wealthy, with animals kept in very small cages with no thought given to their welfare. Thankfully, today all accredited zoos continue making changes to their exhibits in order to educate the public more effectively while improving the quality of life of the animals.

Reid Park Zoo in Tucson is small enough to enjoy in one day without feeling overwhelmed. The continents of Asia, Africa and South America are represented (and there's a polar bear exhibit too), and it's easy to get around on the paved walkways that loop through the various exhibits. The much larger Phoenix Zoo (125 acres) has four main trails—the Africa Trail, the Tropics Trail, the Arizona Trail (with animals from the Sonoran Desert) and the Children's Trail (especially for kids). Because of the zoo's size, it is best enjoyed in segments, so choose different areas each time you visit.

Both zoos have implemented a new practice called "enrichment," whereby the animals are provided with activities (usually involving food) that provide challenge and variety in their daily lives. At Reid Park Zoo, the elephants are given special bins and barrels, filled with treats and chained to a cable, so that they have to flip them around to get their reward. Check the scheduled times when the keepers put these out.

Both locations also help you escape the heat. At Reid Park's "Kenya Get Wet" there is a water pump, a wall spray, and a pond and stream, all cool places for a hot day. Just know that it is a small space and crowding could be a problem. At the Phoenix Zoo, the Yakulla Caverns offer water relief and two slides.

The Phoenix Zoo also features the "Wild Walk," an exercise trail with different exercises at each exhibit. Each exercise relates to the behavior of the animal that it is closest to. These are good ways to get the kids to slow down and use up some of the extra energy. There is a balance beam next to the flamingos, arm hangs and pull-ups next to the orangutans, a drinking fountain by the elephants (with a sign that reads "drink water" and explains that elephants can drink 50 gallons a day. And by the tortoise exhibit there is a sign that says "Relax, enjoy, and slow down." Good advice for any visit to the zoo.

Bonding and bridging:

The excitement that occurs when children see these new, living creatures is contagious and you will remember the thrill you felt the first time you saw an elephant or a giraffe. "Funny," "scary" and "amazing" are all words that describe the sights in the zoo. This experience gives us a chance to talk about nature and the animals that live in the wild. Why are some endangered? And what can we do to help them survive? You may get into a discussion with an older child about the more difficult questions/issues of captivity. Is it right? If so, why? How would the child feel confined to an area like that? Then talk about the newer exhibits and what they like about them.

This is also a great chance to talk about how important it is for us to protect wild areas, so that these animals will always have a place to live in the wild, and not just be found in zoos.

A word to the wise:

All grandparents want to keep their grandchildren in view when we take them to public places, but whenever kids have the opportunity to run ahead, they will, and there is always the possibility of becoming separated from one another, especially in large crowds. There is nothing quite as frightening for adults than to feel as if they've lost a child. Before you begin your exploration of the zoo, discuss a plan of action with your grandchild if they should become separated and can't find you. Choose an exact and easy-to-find location where you will both go, or introduce them to a docent (volunteer) or staff person in a Zoo uniform that they can go to if they can't find you.

Age of grandchild: Toddler–teenager

Best season: Spring or early summer, when there are likely to be more baby animals

Contact: Reid Park Zoo: (520) 791-4022 • www.tucsonzoo.org

Phoenix Zoo: (602) 273-1341 • www.phoenixzoo.org

Also check out:

Wildlife World Zoo & Aquarium: www.wildlifeworld.com

Heritage Park Zoological Sanctuary: www.heritageparkzoo.org

Grandparents, like heroes, are as necessary to a child's growth as vitamins. Joyce Allston

The Mini-Time Machine Museum of Miniatures

When we are children, we live among giants. We stretch high for doorknobs and climb on stools to reach kitchen cabinets, so it is no wonder that we are drawn to miniatures. Toy soldiers, miniature farm sets, tiny tea settings, and doll houses are just a few of the toys that engaged us and fascinate children today. They allow the child to create imaginary worlds and situations where they are in control. As we grow up and the world shrinks in size, many people put aside their miniatures, but not everyone. Some people rediscover them as adults.

As you approach the massive front door of The Mini-Time Machine Museum of Miniatures with its gigantic handle high up on the side and a smaller one that's easier to reach about shoulder height, you know you are about to enter a special world. Inside the entryway, you will hear a twinkling sound; watch the wall to your left for a glowing, twirling image that moves up and into a tiny door on the wall. This is Caitlin, the resident fairy. Every time you hear that twinkling sound, watch for her to skim across a wall or another surface.

The Museum is filled with the private collections of Pat Arnell, her husband, and other collectors. There are three main galleries. The first is filled with glass displays of dollhouses from many ages and countries. It is called "Exploring the World" and by looking at the decorations in the house you can use it to study history and geography. The decorations range from the intricate and ornate to the simple two -shelf glass-fronted cabinet. It takes time to look at each dollhouse and let your eye wander slowly over the details.

A large artificial tree that spreads its branches across the ceiling dominates another large room. Set into the trunk at various levels are little scenes where you can see mice celebrating Christmas. Mice seem to be a favorite character in a lot of the miniature settings throughout this room, along with rabbits and bears. Some of the displays are not in typical houses, but coffee pots, violins, walnuts, straw hats, wooden bird cages. There are Fairy Castles and a big Goldilocks and Three Bears house and a Witches Mansion with all sorts of ghoulish and ghostly characters. In one window display are many music boxes and you can push buttons to play them. In another window kids will be surprised to find a Playmobile dollhouse.

Bonding and bridging:

Playing with toys may be something we grow out of, but it doesn't take much to bring memories flooding back. Some say that as grandparents we go through our second childhood and in a way we do—through our grandchildren. We can (vicariously) feel the thrill of a receiving a new toy and we should have patience and time to engage in play. It's always more fun for the child if you participate in their imaginary world, but if you can't, then many children are content to just have you watch and comment.

Dollhouses are traditionally a girl's toy, but making the furniture for a dollhouse may be one way to engage boys in the world of miniatures. If you are skilled with tools you can help both granddaughters and grandsons make some basic beds, chairs and tables for tiny dolls to use. Remind them that when architects design a building, they first create miniature versions of the building, complete with people and cars and other additional décor.

A word to the wise:

By their nature, many miniatures (except for toy soldiers and Hot Wheels cars) seem to be geared to girls. Boys will probably enjoy the Enchanted Room, with its emphasis on fantasy—dragons, castles and Halloween characters. With that said, there really aren't any interactive exhibits and so they will have a limited time until they become bored. This is mostly a "look, don't touch" museum, so you will have to decide if your grandchild is one who will enjoy spending time carefully looking into all the many dollhouse creations and all the tiny décor used in them. Very small children will have a hard time seeing into the displays and your arms will grow weary lifting them up and down.

Age of grandchild: 5 and older

Best season: Any

Contact: 4455 E Camp Lowell Drive, Tucson, AZ 85712 • (520) 881-0606
• www.theminitimemachine.org

Also check out:

Arizona Doll and Toy Museum: www.azcama.com/museums/doll_toy.html

Tucson Children's Museum: www.tucsonchildrensmuseum.org

Arizona Museum for Youth: www.arizonamuseumforyouth.com

Grandchildren are the dots that connect the lines from generation to generation. Lois Wyse

Saguaro National Park and Arizona-Sonora Desert Museum

It is hard to separate these two places, in fact, it is hard to tell where one ends and the next begins, but together they encompass the saguaro cacti that appear to march along the mountain ridge like an army of green Kachina dolls. Saguaro National Park is a Sonoran reserve that consists of two parts that surround Tucson. From the Rincon Mountains on the East to the Tucson Mountains on the West, the city of Tucson sits in a valley, part of a larger geological region known as the Basin and Range.

Depending on the age of your grandchildren there are many ways to explore this region. One is to hike. There are great trails in the National Park as well as at the city park and these trails not only wander through the rugged mountain rocks, but up and down the flanks that geologists call bajadas (Spanish for "shoulders"). Or you can stop by the National Park Visitor Center where a slide presentation will tell you about the landscape and the inspiration it has been to people over thousands of years. You can look at the displays, observe from the deck, and talk to the interpretive staff to plan adventures and explorations.

On bikes, you can ride to the west half of Saguaro and cover the eight-mile-long loop on a roller coaster road that takes you in and out of flash flood valleys and up on the side of the mountain before finishing with a nice downhill ride. And if that is not enough to get the desert sands stirring in your heart and mind, there is the Arizona-Sonora Desert Museum which is a world-famous zoo, botanical garden and natural history museum.

The animals you come to observe may actually stop by to observe you. Instead of creating all new exhibits and enclosures, the Museum incorporated the existing landscape. Within it, you and your grandchildren can observe the wild cats, and try to find the javelina and coyotes as they blend with their enclosure. You can also walk through a cave and see cave formations, as well as a mining exhibit. Another room is filled with exhibits of snakes and lizards, as well as some unique desert insect life. Go through the controlled entrance of the aviary and suddenly you join the birds inside their exhibit. Best of all (we are biased!) is the hummingbird enclosure where you and these feathered jewels can come eye to eye around feeders and flowers. Use this to prepare for your trips into the field where you can look for the birds in their natural habitat.

Bonding and bridging:

If you want your grandchildren to learn, demonstrate that you enjoy learning! Think of the indirect lessons of life: if a child never sees an adult open a book, the lesson is that books are only for children.

The National Park offers naturalist programs and the Desert Museum has educational stations (with docents) spread throughout the exhibits. These are simple and short, but they are interesting and challenging lessons where we can learn with our grandchild at our side. We can celebrate new knowledge and let them know how important learning is. This will help them learn about the museum, but it is a lesson that has much greater implications.

In the fall, the museum hosts a Butterfly Festival to investigate the population of winged wonders and the National Park has an annual American Indian Cultural Fair.

A word to the wise:

This really is the desert. No kidding! The sun is hot and hats make a difference. We dry out from sweating and from breathing and the loss of body fluids can change our feelings and our attitude. Prevent this by staying hydrated and choose a mix of both water and a flavored beverage that contains the little miracle minerals called electrolytes that help with our body chemistry and balance. If you consume liquid regularly you will be happier, have more energy, and suffer fewer headaches and muscle fatigue. A lot of salt is not necessary, but a little salt in an energy bar is another way to balance the loss that occurs when we sweat.

Age of grandchild: 8 and up

Best season: Fall, winter, spring

Contact: Saguaro National Park: 3693 Old Spanish Trail, Tucson, AZ 85730 • (520) 733-5158 (west) • (520) 733-5153 (east) • www.nps.gov/sagu

Arizona-Sonora Desert Museum: 2021 N Kinney Road, Tucson, AZ 85743 • (520) 883-3082 • www.desertmuseum.org

Also check out:

Organ Pipe Cactus National Monument: www.nps.gov/orpi

Tohono Chul Park: www.tohonochulpark.org

Grandparents are similar to a piece of string—handy to have around and easily wrapped around the fingers of their grandchildren. UNKNOWN

33

Biosphere 2

The white glass-covered domes pop out of the desert like an alien settlement on the moon, and in some ways this was an alien experiment. In 1991, eight men and women (equally divided by gender) chose to enter this facility for two years of separation from the outside world, as if they were leaving for an extraterrestrial journey. The goal of the undertaking was to see whether humans could in fact recreate a biosphere (this is what the earth is) that could sustain life. This would be a good test to see whether we could transport our life systems to another planet. It was an interesting, and ultimately unsuccessful, experiment. The eight people survived, but lost weight, energy and patience with one another. The Biosphere itself lost oxygen—eight tons of it. At its worst it was the equivalent of living at 17,000 feet. The scientists in the group couldn't figure out where the oxygen had gone, because the Biosphere was airtight. Then they realized that the organic matter in their soil had introduced microbes that began to consume large quantities of this life-sustaining gas.

Since the end of the experiment, Biosphere 2 has been owned and managed by Columbia University and now by the University of Arizona. Just the appearance of this complex will intrigue the children. Older kids will be able to understand more of the science that the guide explains, but everyone will be fascinated by the idea of trying to live for two years in this self-contained setting. Aboveground, the Biosphere covers three acres. Below ground is the "technospere"—two acres of mechanical equipment that keeps the entire system operating. The facility itself was designed to replicate five biomes found on our planet: rainforest, desert, ocean, estuary or marsh, and savannah. If you have been missing the feeling of humid air, you will rediscover it the moment you walk into the glass covered building where the tours begin. This is after all basically a giant greenhouse. You will walk through and past all of the biomes, and your guide will explain what was done originally and what is being done now to try to better understand our natural world. One of the last places you will visit is the "technospere." It is called the lung and is an engineering marvel. I won't spoil the ending, but let's just say that your grandchildren will get a surprise thrill when they leave this location.

Bonding and bridging:

This tour presents a lot of tough questions related to climate change, and not a lot of answers. But science is about asking questions and testing out hypotheses. Children are natural-born scientists. They are always questioning their surroundings. We should encourage that curiosity, because we need these children to grow up and find challenge and reward in science, as well as be knowledgeable enough to know how to question data that is presented to them. The US used to be a leader in science, but that has changed in recent years and other countries are surpassing us in the number of mathematicians, physicists and other natural science professionals they produce. If we want our grandchildren to live in a country as successful as the one we have known, we must encourage them to pursue scientific study. It might be fun to find some books on science fiction to read or listen to on CD together after visiting this "far out" and futuristic facility.

A word to the wise:

It will be hot and humid in the building. Bring a hat, since the sun shines through 6,500 windows. Wear comfortable shoes and be prepared to go up and down steps and ramps. If you are skeptical about climate change, be prepared to hear a lot of discussion of this topic, since much of the research that occurs at the Biosphere now is focused on its affect on plants and the various ecosystems. The guides are respectful of everyone's opinion.

Age of grandchild: 6 and older

Best season: Anytime, but winter is probably the best because of temperatures within the facility

Contact: 32540 S Biosphere Road, Oracle, AZ 85623 • (520) 838-6200 • www.b2science.org

Also check out:

Arcosanti and Cosanti: www.arcosanti.org/expCosanti

Frank Lloyd Wright's Taliesin West: www.franklloydwright.org

Pima Air and Space Museum

Think of a used car lot of vintage airplanes spread over acres of creosote desert and you get an idea of the setting for the Pima Air and Space Museum and its multiple hangers and building. This is the third-largest air museum in the nation and it is not a place where you can just spend an hour and feel satisfied. Commit the time needed to explore with your grandchildren. Let them look, ask questions, and settle into exploring. Sometimes places like this can be so overwhelming that it takes time for children to adjust.

This place is huge—so pace yourself and realize that you cannot look at all 275 different aircraft in one visit. Explore, sit and take a break, and then explore some more. It is made easier because the exhibit is broken up into four hangars, a WWII barracks, the space gallery and a separate Memorial Museum for the 390th Bomb Group. All of this is included in the price of admission, as is the boneyard—the outdoor exhibit of planes that really demonstrates the variety and creativity of aircraft design. There are two alternatives to a long outdoor hike among the aircraft in the sun. One is a tram tour that lasts an hour and includes some narration about the aircraft and helps you avoid the heat. Your grandchildren will like the ride, but may not stay attentive all the way through. A motorcoach tour is another option. It also lasts an hour. This tour takes you to the aircraft maintenance and regeneration group at Davis-Monthan Air Force Base. If your grandkids like model planes, they'll REALLY like seeing life-sized planes.

Back at the museum, the first building is the place to take smaller kids, as they'll be able to climb into cockpits, do puzzles, and explore a runway surveillance unit. This works well since it allows the kids to get out some of their post-drive need to move and play and then you can walk, talk and explore. Don't miss the 390th Bomb Group Memorial, dedicated to veterans from WWII. The memorial features some dramatic displays about prisoners of war and bombing missions, and it honors the men for their amazing sacrifices. Finally, be sure to visit the space exhibit. We love the way it blends science fiction into the exhibits because what is real today was science fiction during our childhoods. There is also excellent information on the planets and all the missions to our solar system with models, a moon rock, and videos.

Bonding and bridging:

Another place the kids will like is the WWII barracks. This can be a surprise because it is not a building filled with beds, but rather a very large display of model airplanes. Even with the large and real planes parked outside, the kids often relate to things on their own scale (or things that occur on the scale of toys). If they can find models of the planes they've seen at the museum, that's even better. Remember that you are trying to focus on the kid's-eye-view as you wander through the museum.

You might want to consider using this as inspiration to purchase a model airplane to construct with your grandchildren after the tour. It will reinforce what they learned, give them hands-on experience, help augment their coordination, teach them to follow instructions, and help them pay attention to the details of the planes.

A word to the wise:

There are guided hikes through the facilities, but these are more geared to adults than children. When you bring the grandchildren, they should be the focus. But that does not mean that you can't interact with the volunteers. In fact, it would be terrible if you missed the discussions that you can have with these dedicated and very intelligent people. They have stories to tell and you should engage them; the grandchildren will respond to these in a one-on-one conversation much better than in a group setting. One fun anecdote we listened to had to do with the conversion of Air Force One from a propeller-powered plane to jet-driven one. This occurred during the Eisenhower administration; they had to keep the propeller-driven plane, as well, through the Johnson presidency in order to land at smaller airports.

Age of grandchild: 3 and up

Best season: Any time

Contact: 6000 E Valencia Road, Tucson, AZ 85756-9403 • (520) 574-0462 • www.pimaair.org • www.390th.org

Also check out:

CAF Aviation Museum, Mesa: www.azcaf.org

Planes of Fame Air Museum, Valle-Williams: www.planesoffame.org

Titan Missile Museum Green Valley: www.titanmissilemuseum.org

It's amazing how grandparents seem so young once you become one. Unknown

Eyes On the Sky

A visit to a mountaintop observatory is almost a trip to space itself. Winding, twisting mountain roads move from desert to forest and finally to the realm of the sky. Large telescopes and observatories are perched at the top of the isolated peaks of Arizona and search the stars for a variety of scientific purposes.

On a sunny day the drive up Kitt Peak is filled with distant views across the basins and ranges that make this landscape famous. Going around the switch-

backs you glimpse circular buildings rising like mushrooms from the peak. Not one white building, but one after the other. These buildings have no counterpart in the urban centers of the basins. They are meant to peer into outer space, but they look like they might have originated there.

There are guided hikes if your grandchildren are really interested in space exploration, or self-guided walks if you want to control the time and pace. Kitt Peak is just one of the places where astronomers work, but it is also one of the most impressive places on earth because there are 26 scopes. One telescope, in particular, searches for potential asteroids and meteors that might collide with earth. The radio telescope is coordinated with listening devices around the continent, and the strange building that looks like an office tower that broke off and fell over is a solar telescope that captures the energy and image of the sun so we can trace solar storms that sometimes wreak havoc with our communication systems.

You cannot peer into the scopes, but you can go into the buildings and look at these amazing instruments and compare them with the rather small telescope Galileo used to see the moons of Jupiter. In the visitor center you can see yourself on TV as an infrared camera traces your movements, or sit in the video room and look at some of the latest observations.

The Lowell Observatory in Flagstaff does not have as dramatic a setting, but it has a tremendous history. Here the visitor center has interactive kiosks that provide great insight for every family member. Explore your knowledge of space together before taking the guided tour through some of the historic buildings where Percival Lowell began studying the "canals" of Mars in hopes of finding Martians. (These canals ended up being natural structures.) While Martians weren't located, Pluto was discovered here and the observatory and its related telescopes have produced other important astronomical knowledge.

Bonding and bridging:

Often the only things our grandchildren know about space originated on TV or in the movies. There is so much more they can relate to. Take your grandchild to a dark sky location (these are getting rare) and look at the skies. Learn a few of the mythological tales and share them. Find the easy constellations, then use binoculars if you lack a telescope. Create an opportunity for space exploration.

There are also observing options at all the observatories, but they are costly and must be reserved in advance. You can also buy sky charts and get calendars that list meteor showers and other good sky shows. And you can always look at the moon with your binoculars. Above all, let your grandchild know that night is not evil; it is only the bad choices that some people make that give darkness a bad reputation.

A word to the wise:

Even using binoculars to look at the moon can open up vistas for the grandchildren. When they see the craters on the moon, it is no longer a piece of cheese in the sky, but rather a real place, one that has had the footprints of a limited number of people. They need to know that real life adventure is actually much more compelling than the fictional space literature and movies, but they will not know that unless you help them. Who can predict where science will take this new generation of children? If your grandchild shows real interest, both Lowell and Kitt Peak have overnight viewing experiences. You might start with evening experiences on Mount Lemmon or attend an astronomy talk. You have the gift of a universe to present to your grandchild, it doesn't get any bigger than that.

Age of grandchild: 8 and up, but it's best to start at the earliest age

Best season: Winter has the clearest skies, but visit any time of year

Contact: Kitt Peak National Observatory and Museum: (520) 318-8726 • www.noao.edu/outreach/kpoutreach.html

Lowell Observatory: 1400 West Mars Hill Road, Flagstaff, AZ 86001 • www.lowell.edu • (928) 774-3358

Also check out:

University of AZ and Steward Observatory, Tucson: www.as.arizona.edu

Father Kino's Mission Road

The story of southern Arizona begins with the Pima people (O'odham) living on the sparse offerings of the desert landscape. They were a peaceful people who knew how to irrigate and grow crops like beans, corn and squash, but they were vulnerable to attacks from a tribe from the north, the Apache. Then the Spanish arrived, promising protection from the Apache, but for a price. The Spanish brought along their soldiers and missionaries. Soon they settled the area and occupied from present-day Tumacacori National Monument to the Presidio of Tucson.

Father Eusebio Kino was a Jesuit who came here in 1691, intent on bringing his beliefs to the people of this continent. Today you can visit many important places where the cultures of Spain, Mexico, Pima, and Apache intersected. Many of these locations were influenced by Father Kino, and today constitute something of a "mission road." Start at Tumacacori and work north. In the first location watch the park video and explore the museum before taking the walk through the ruins. This will give all of you a better knowledge of the history and what the old buildings stand for. You can also walk into the ancient sanctuary and feel the sense of purpose and sanctity that was put into the construction of this place of worship.

Move north to Tubac and you can visit the first state park in Arizona. Exhibits tell the story of a location that rose from obscurity to importance and back to obscurity and, maybe, back to success. The old Presidio walls are mostly gone and the old road is a depression in the ground, but here was the first European settlement in the region, the first newspaper, and even the origin of the expedition that founded San Francisco. Can you imagine? Talk about the idea that such important things can happen anywhere.

The final stop along this mission route is San Xavier del Bac which is also located in the Santa Cruz Valley near outcroppings of volcanic rock and the homes of the San Xavier reservation. You can walk around the mission, an active church, and marvel at its history and perseverance. Tell your grandchildren that the name means "place where the water appears" and ask them if the place has changed since Father Kino was here in 1692. Walk along the plaza, compare the towers and see which one is older. Walk up the hill and see the shrines and then don't forget to visit the mission school.

Bonding and bridging:

Father Kino was born in Italy in 1645. He renounced his minor nobility to come to North America and serve the church. By 1687 he was assigned to work with the Pima and he took the time to learn the Pima way of life and traveled throughout the Pima region for 24 years. The soldiers and settlers in the area were from Spain. Imagine how this must have seemed to the Indians who lived here. How would it feel if you lived here when an army came and said your home belonged to them? Then again, in history it is important to understand stories from all sides. Many times there are good people on both sides of a conflict.

And while we know history is written by the victors, it's important to explore all sides of the story. We can ask who the original inhabitants of this area were, how they lived, and what kind of people they were. These are tough perspectives that we all have to grapple with as we grow older and wiser.

A word to the wise:

In the courtyard at Tumacacori there is a ocotillo-roofed ramada that often has a special treat that you should check out. For years Gloria Moroyoqui has made homemade tortillas on a wood-fired stove and served them with her own fresh pinto beans, cheese and salsa. There is no charge for this cultural bonus that is both fascinating and delicious. Try them with your grandchildren, challenge them to taste this treat even if they are reluctant. Then watch her make the tortilla, watch it cook and talk about the different ways that we cook in our kitchens today and how your grandmother would have cooked.

Age of grandchild: 7 and up

Best season: Fall, winter, spring

Contact: Tumacacori National Historical Park: PO Box 8067, Tumacacori, AZ 85640 • (520) 398-2341 • www.nps.gov/tuma

Tubac Presidio State Historic Park: PO Box 1296, Tubac, AZ 85646 • (520) 398-2252 • www.azstateparks.com/parks/tupr

Also check out: Mission San Xavier del Bac, Franciscan Friars: 1950 W San Xavier Road, Tucson, AZ 85746 • (520) 294-2624 • www.sanxaviermission.org

If I had known how wonderful it would be to have grandchildren, I'd have had them first. LOIS WYSE

Patagonia-Sonoita Creek Preserve, Patagonia Lake State Park and Sonoita Creek Natural Area

The Patagonia-Sonoita Creek Preserve, Patagonia Lake State Park and Sonoita Creek Natural Area are all natural areas that are related and occur right next to one another, but they are also quite different and complement one another.

Patagonia Lake State Park features a freshwater lake (a manmade impoundment) while Patagonia-Sonoita Creek Preserve is the early stage of a free-flowing stream before the park and Sonoita Creek Natural Area is the natural valley after the park. All three of these locations are part of the most famous bird watching area in the US. The lake is the focus of the State Park. There is a picnic area, a campground and a swimming beach for recreation. You can fish, stop at the visitor center and take one of the scheduled pontoon boat rides, or you can hike the trails and look for the birds that frequent deeper water. Ancient Indian petroglyphs can be seen on one shore, and on the other you can find a store for a cold treat and a marina where you can rent a canoe or rowboat. If you run out of things to do, there is a ranger program too; head over to the visitor center for a schedule.

On the other side of the State Park is the Sonoita Creek Natural Area with trails to explore this free flowing stream and large trees to provide shade and shelter for bird and hiker alike. There is a regular schedule of bird hikes led by local experts and you can see which ones would welcome kids. This is an excellent way to find the specialties of the valley.

Located near the city of Patagonia, the Patagonia-Sonoita Creek Preserve belongs to the Nature Conservancy, with a visitor center to help orient you. Just outside the Preserve is Marion Paton's home where bird watchers have congregated for years to enjoy one of the world's most exciting hummingbird concentrations. The hummingbirds are drawn in by birdfeeders, and you can sit and watch or photograph these extraordinary avian sprites! Check the website to double-check the hours and availability.

Bonding and bridging:

Have you heard the word "bioblitz?" It describes a way to take a quick survey of a natural area. You don't have to know all the plants, insects, mammals, birds, etc., but it is a way to see how many different kinds there are. This is something you can do with your grandchild. Create a list and choose any format you want to list all the different things you see. Just list the number of trees, flowers, grasses, birds, etc., that you see.

After you've completed your first one, you can compare it with other bioblitzes you complete at different times of day, in different locations, and so on. You can do this wherever you go on hikes and it will help your grandchild to see and expect diversity. It is the beginning of a background in ecology and a way to start wonderful discussions. Make predictions, keep lists, make comparisons. Everything that extends an experience is a good thing for you and your grandchildren. Learning is part of having fun and builds a wonderful future.

A word to the wise:

Patagonia is a lake-based State Park and boats can be a big part of the experience here. If your grandchild likes boats you can get a boating safety coloring book from the visitor center. Make sure you help them to see the valuable safety information. Make it fun, not a lecture. This kind of knowledge is very important for their future and can add to the fun if you have access to a boat. You can also go the park's website and download Junior Ranger information for kids 6–12 years old.

Age of grandchild: All, depending on the activities you choose

Best season: Spring and summer for bird watching; all seasons otherwise

Contact: Patagonia Lake State Park: 400 Patagonia Lake Road, Patagonia, AZ 85624 • http://azstateparks.com/Parks/PALA

Nature Conservancy's Patagonia-Sonoita Creek Preserve: www.nature.org/wherewework/northamerica/states/arizona/preserves/art1972.html

Sonoita Creek State Natural Area: http://azstateparks.com/Parks/SOCR/index.html

Also check out:

Marion Paton Hummingbird Backyard: www.sonoitacreek.com/Marion_Paton_Backyard_Feeders.html

On the Trail of Hummingbirds

Arizona is the land of bird watchers. Busloads of binocular-toting grandparents, biologists, bird watchers, tourists and outdoor enthusiasts descend upon the 'Sky Islands' and all their unique habitats each year to look for the rare and the beautiful. Like modern-day gunfighters, they are ready to raise their binoculars and take aim at the slightest movement. Can you share the excitement of this hunt with your grandchild and give them a lifetime hobby?

We set out bird feeders at our home to keep the birds close and active as we sit, eat or play on the deck, and we especially like to have hummingbird feeders to attract this very tiny, fast and fascinating group of birds. In Minnesota where we live, we only get to see the ruby-throated hummingbird, but in Arizona it is possible to see up to 17 hummingbird species. Kids love the motion, the sound and even the aggressiveness that the birds display as they fight for the feeder openings. And the good thing is that the birds will keep coming back to the feeders all day. All of this makes it the perfect activity to get little people watching little birds and get children hooked on bird watching.

Your search for hummingbirds will take you to beautiful places like the Santa Rita Mountains and the Arizona-Sonora Desert Museum. At Ramsey Canyon, the visitor center has large posters on the wall that describe the species and help with the identification. Let them look at these and at the birds as they feed, then help them to find the birds in a field guide. Learning how to use field guides is one of the two essential skills required for bird watching success.

The second skill is using binoculars. Even adults have difficulty finding birds, butterflies, even billboards with binoculars. Like every tool we use, we need to practice using them. To use the gunfighter analogy again, when using binoculars you have to be quick on draw and fast on focus. That means we have to be able to put the binoculars in front of our eyes without taking our focus off the bird. That is easier said than done. Hummingbird feeders are a great place to start since the feeders are stationary. If you can find and focus on birds visiting on feeders, you'll be rewarded over and over.

Bonding and bridging:

You can begin to teach your grandchild how to recognize and identify birds before they ever see one in the wild. Kate has flash cards that she uses when she visits the grandchildren. They love the challenge of naming things. It is a game for them, but one that contributes to real knowledge. We also have a placemat with local birds displayed and we challenge them at meal times. It is about repetition and reinforcement. No penalty for getting it wrong, but lots of praise when you get it right.

It is always a good idea to point out nature's own bird feeders—the flowers that hummingbirds are attracted to. Together you can come up with some ideas for plants to put into your own garden to attract birds and even butterflies, which add another dimension to any garden. Like hummingbirds, butterflies are sure to delight children and add even more color to a garden.

A word to the wise:

In the spring, the birds are at the peak of their color and the males are aggressive and display a lot. In the late summer and early fall, the young hummingbirds are out of their nests and this is when we get more action as the family grows from 2 birds to 6 or 8 and then they all have to compete for the precious liquid food! In the fall, since there are more hummingbirds, the birds consume more nectar, so be prepared to refill the feeders regularly. Fill them with a 1:4 mixture of sugar to water, but don't put a dye in it. The liquid does not have to be red, as the feeder already is. Finally, do not let the liquid sit out for more than two days. In hot temperatures the sugar solution can quickly breed harmful bacteria.

Age of grandchild: 2 and up

Best season: Spring migration, mid-April through September

Contact: Ramsey Canyon Nature Preserve: (520) 378-2785

Arizona-Sonora Desert Museum, Tucson: www.desertmuseum.org

Also check out:

Southeastern Arizona Bird Observatory, San Pedro River: www.sabo.org

Tohono Chul Park, Tucson: www.tohonochulpark.org

Kartchner Caverns

When the sun is high and the mountains are hot you might reason as we did—this would be a good time to explore a cave. Time to get out of the sun, drop into the cool region below the surface, maybe even put on a sweatshirt!

You can do this at Kartchner Caverns State Park, but be prepared for surprises, because this very unique cave is both warm and humid.

Carved out of a downthrust section of the Whetstone Mountain group, this low-elevation limestone layer has been dissolved by carbonic acid deposited by rainwater over the eons. When it was discovered in 1974 it was a refuge for bats and little else. Fortunately the spelunkers (cave explorers) who discovered this cave were aware of what happened to so many unprotected caves around the world and they worked to keep it a secret and to get formal protection.

Now you and your grandchildren can benefit from this effort. Beginning in the visitor center, you can explore the world of caves. A guide will greet you outside in a small area where you will begin to learn that this is more than a walk through a dark tunnel. You will learn what "basin and range" means and start to understand how water works within an arid climate.

A tram will bring you up to the entrance of the cave. The real entrance is a sinkhole on the side of the foothill, but you will walk up to an entrance created by miners who used their tools and skill to create a winding, level entry and a sealed set of corridors where humans can shed their microbes and foreign material from the world of the surface.

In the first of two large rooms, the guide will direct your attention to the formations and explain how they came to be. Entering the second and last chamber you will see the best of the best and it will help you understand why at least one publication puts this in the top ten mineralogy caves in the world. All the colors, the forms, and the rocks are perfect because of the long history of deformation, metamorphism and cave deposits. Here you will see soda straws on stalactites, ribbons and curtains, towers and stalagmites. But now I have to warn you: the next sentence gives away a little of the climactic ending, so you might want to stop right here! In the last room poetry and music combine as Kubla Khan and Xanadu formations become a part of the final movement in this educational immersion and it is terrific.

Bonding and bridging:

Entering an alien landscape together is a bonding experience. Nothing in our terrestrial landscape prepares us for the world beneath the surface. The movement of water is a sign of growth and activity. It is the pulse of the cave and it tells you that it is still active and you are just visiting it during its long lifetime. This a good opportunity to talk about what makes us comfortable and uncomfortable. Where do we feel best? Where do we go to be inspired?

There is a nice little snack bar where you can buy something refreshing and then you can sit on the benches in the wonderful butterfly garden that is planted around the visitor center. It is a beautiful native plant garden, which attracts gorgeous birds. In this hot, dry land it offers the unique experience of sitting in the shade!

A word to the wise:

You need not worry about footing in the cavern, since everything is paved and handicap accessible. The lights help keep the cave from becoming a "scary darkness," but it will still be an alien landscape that will challenge the child's comfort zone (and maybe yours too).

When you are in the 99% humidity of the cave you pick up moisture on your clothes and your skin. Then when you step outside into the hotter, dryer air, the moisture on your body will evaporate and you will feel as if you are being cooled, if only for a short time.

Keep this in mind should you decide to walk the Loop Trail. You will be exposed to the sun and you need to check the temperature and be prepared. It is a wonderful walk, but has a lot of loose rocks that can be a problem depending upon your balance and vision.

Age of grandchild: 7 and up

Best season: Any

Contact: PO Box 1849, Benson, AZ 85602 • Reservation Line: (520) 586-2283 • Information Line: (520) 586-4100 • www.azstateparks.com/parks/kaca

Also check out:

Grand Canyon Caverns: www.gccaverns.com

Grandparents somehow sprinkle a sense of stardust over grandchildren. Alex Haley

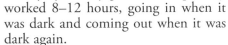

Copper Mines and Minerals

Copper is the color of Arizona in many ways. The bronze hue is in the sunsets, on the dome of the historic capitol, and in the history of the state and its economics. Copper has caused men to spend most of their lives underground working by candle, carbide lamp, and finally by battery-powered lamp. They

worked 8–12 hours, going in when it was dark and coming out when it was dark again.

No town has more history in copper than Bisbee where the hills are honeycombed with mines and the city resides in a narrow canyon perched beside mesas created by the tailings (waste) from the mines. Bisbee's winding streets are now filled with art and tourist shops but the old Dodge Phelps office beneath the Copper Queen has a museum that tells the story of copper through displays and artifacts that will help you and your grandchildren understand what you will see and experience.

The historic tour of the Queen Mines is an underground experience that the kids will like because everyone must put on a slicker, a hard hat, a miner's belt and a battery and a light before sitting on the small train that takes you into the shafts to explore the life of a hard rock miner. It was a tough life that is usually described by someone who actually lived it. The mine is cold, it is claustrophobic (dark and close) and your grandchildren may need to be reassured. It is not a trip that they should take unless they are interested in rocks, history and an unusual adventure. The same is true for the grandparent. The light that is hung over their neck will be intriguing and they will love to explore the dark with it.

They will be tested by the length of some presentations. These are old miners, not professional speakers and they are telling their story, but it might not entertain the children. If you want to experience the scale of mining, you only have to go a short distance to the open pit viewing station, but it'd be better to drive to an active mining operation with tours that will get you close to the action and the kids can see the large equipment as well as the large open mine.

Bonding and bridging:

We are responsible for what we choose, including what we buy and throw away. While the beauty of the raw earth and the colors of the open pit are fascinating, the pit and the holes in the earth also represent our quest to fulfill our perceived needs and demands. Here it is important to talk about the choices we make. The average family, according to the Morenci Mine, has 440 pounds of copper in their home. Copper is used for many important products where nothing else works as well. When we use copper poorly or we throw it away instead of recycling it, we create the demand to dig larger holes and process more raw materials. In the Morenci Mine, 700,000 tons of rock are removed each day. That is 1,400,000,000 pounds of rock, 365 days a year. Do the math and see how much we are changing the earth. 840,000,000 pounds of copper a year are produced by the Morenci Mines. Compare that total with the total rock per year.

A word to the wise:

Do some rock collecting to help the children see the beauty in our raw earth. Kids love to touch how rocks feel, and most of the mines and museums do not allow this, so add rock collecting to your list of family adventures. Start a collection that is based on stories so that when each rock is picked up it brings to mind a time of sharing.

Age of grandchild: 6 and up

Best season: Any

Contact: Queen Mine Tour: 478 N Dart Road, Bisbee, AZ 85603 • (866) 432-2071 or (520) 432-2071 • www.queenminetour.com

ASARCO Mineral Discovery Center: 1421 W Pima Mine Road, Sahuarita, AZ 85629 • (520) 625-7513 • www.mineraldiscovery.com

Bisbee Mining and Historical Museum: 5 Copper Queen Plaza, Bisbee, AZ 85540 • (520) 432-7071 • www.bisbeemuseum.org

Also check out:

Arizona Mining and Mineral Museum, Phoenix: www.admmr.state.az.us/General/museum.html

University of Arizona Mineral Museum: www.uamineralmuseum.org

I've learned that when your newly born grandchild holds your little finger in his fist, that you're hooked for life. ANDY ROONEY

49

Tombstone

The billboard claims that Tombstone is "too tough to die," but its longevity might be due to a gunfight too spectacular to forget and all the movies that keep dramatizing it. A National Historic Landmark that is considered one of the best preserved 1870–1880 frontier towns, Tombstone also has a colorful name with a colorful past and it will continue to lure visitors far into the future. For grandchildren it is a look back to the television and movie mythology that affected their grandparents when they were children.

This was a silver mining town, one that was so violent President Chester A. Arthur threatened to send in troops to calm things down. The newspaper ran a regular column called "Death's Doings." Today the town's primary economy is not mining, but tourism and it is based on the image of the West that people still enjoy—the legends, the exaggerations, and even outright lies.

As far as Tombstone's tourism reputation is concerned, the gunfight at the O.K. Corral on October 26, 1881, established the cornerstone of this historic industry. The fight featured thirty shots in thirty seconds, and thanks to that fight, and others like it, there are men and women walking in costume, their minds set in the Old West.

Fittingly, it was a movie that gave the town its motto—Tombstone, The Town Too Tough To Die (1942). One town historian claims at least 25 gunfight related movies have been released since. Watching one might be a good thing to do with your grandchild and add to the visit, especially if you help them understand how these stories are for entertainment, not history. Stagecoaches and covered wagons give rides down the main street with characters dressed for the location and the 1880s. There are no sidewalks on Main Street, but boardwalks lead people past old-time stores and saloons. The old Bird Cage Opera House anchors one end of town. Music and color invite you into the saloons and the O.K. Corral does regular reenactments that draw in thousands of intrigued visitors.

And while the history isn't entirely accurate, or even close, this blending of real and the imaginary is part of the charm. It means that our imagination and desires are as much a part of the reality as anything else on the street.

Bonding and bridging:

What makes right and wrong? After all these years there is still controversy about who was the aggressor in the conflict at the O.K. Corral; the facts bear out that neither side was perfect, but the winners have gone on to gain fame. Does winning make someone right? Where do we separate bullying from conflict? These are issues that every child faces and perhaps they fantasize about getting even, but is that right?

Here is a situation where you can talk about some issues that are important, but difficult to approach. This is where we can talk about the advancements we have made, and the fact that not everyone wants to work at good solutions. What was it like for the non-violent people who lived in Tombstone? What would it have been like for the children? Can we know the stories behind the violence and the death?

A word to the wise:

This is a tourist town and the shops are here to make money. That means that in addition to atmosphere, your grandchild is going to be faced with the temptation to spend money. If you are here for atmosphere and do not want to go broke, it is best to talk about limitations before you arrive, rather than trying to adjust in the midst of temptation. An allowance, or a talk about the reasons that you are here will help. How do children learn limits? This is a start. If you are Old West fanatics, you might want to join the Old West Founders Days in April for parades, petting zoos, variety shows, dancers and performances.

Age of grandchild: 6 12

Best season: April, for the Founders Days celebration, otherwise spring and fall; make your visit in the morning before the heat of the desert day

Contact: Tombstone, AZ: www.tombstone.org • (888) 457-3929

Also check out:

Tombstone Chamber of Commerce: www.tombstonechamber.com

Tombstone Historic District: http://tps.cr.nps.gov/nhl/detail.cfm?resourceid =88&resourcetype=district

Wyatt Earp House & Gallery: www.wyattearphouse.com

Wickenburg: www.outwickenburgway.com

The real mystery of life is not a problem to be solved, it is a reality to be experienced. J.J. Van der Leeuw

Chiricahua National Monument

Imagine a landscape littered with towers and spires molded into shapes that cry out for a name. Occurring at elevations of about 7,000 feet and all the way down into the valley the towers seem to be marching towards the Monument headquarters.

Called "hoodoos" by some, these natural sculptures seem to be more than remnants of an old volcanic ash flow—they are spiritual touchstones to our imagination. The roads give you a good view of the rock formations, but remember that grandchildren are strapped in by car seats, and seatbelts limit their movement and ability to see out the windows. They have to get out to experience both the size and scope of this amazing mountainside.

The easiest hike for the younger child, or if you have impairments, is the interpretive hike at Massai point. The trail is at an elevation of 7,000 feet so the air is thin and even though the trail is mostly flat and short, you will have to judge your own abilities. From up here you can look down onto the community of rock towers, and on the trail you will get a sense of their size.

If you have more time and energy, the Echo Canyon trail is an intimate landscape and there is an area called the Grotto a half mile from the start of the trail where grandkids can scramble on the rocks. It is downhill to this location, so you will have more work hiking back out.

Lizards and birds add variety and excitement to the trip and coatimundis can be seen quite often in quiet areas or near the campground. A quieter hike, both short and flat, can be taken at Faraway Ranch where the Erickson family lived for 91 years. Imagine what life would have been like in this quiet valley surrounded by such inspirational scenery. Are the ranchers of Faraway Ranch part of the spirits that reside in this surreal surroundings? Or are the quiet sighs of the wind in the pines the sounds of the Chiricahua Apaches? Massai Point is named for an Apache warrior, who was chased to the point that now bears his name and then disappeared never to be found again. Is it his spirit that accompanies us on our adventures?

Bonding and bridging:

A place like Chiricahua inspires us in different ways. If your grandchild likes to draw, let them sketch the strange shapes they see here. If you have clay, they can make models of the hoodoos, and if you trust your grandchild with a camera, they can take photos to show you what they see.

Because we have experienced more of life than our grandchildren, our views are tempered, but our grandchildren are not limited by what they have heard and seen. They are seeing the world with fresh eyes and we need to explore their perspective as well as share our own.

A place like this is so refreshingly different that it allows us to talk about what we see and think. It is a way for us to share viewpoints when no one is right or wrong. That equality is fun and enlightening. Make the most of that and record those thoughts at the end of this book!

A word to the wise:

Because the trails head downhill, it is easy to overestimate our abilities, so use restraint when walking down the main trail or when considering the longer trail routes. Be aware that this is a hot region and sometimes the elevation and wind can be deceptive. In addition, at high elevations we are exposed to more of the sun's ultraviolet rays and we can sunburn before we realize it.

Dehydration is also a concern. The combination of the high elevation and a low humidity level means we lose water through perspiration as well as respiration. It is essential to stay hydrated and to consume liquids with an appropriate level of electrolytes.

Age of grandchild: 5 and up

Best season: Spring or fall

Contact: 12856 E Rhyolite Creek Road, Willcox, AZ 85643 • (520) 824-3560 ext. 302 • www.nps.gov/chir/index.htm

Also check out:

Monument Valley Navajo Tribal Park, Kayenta: www.navajonationparks.org/htm/monumentvalley.htm

Tonto Natural Bridge State Park, Pine: http://azstateparks.com/Parks/tona

Rock Collecting in Arizona

Rocks, rocks, rocks, everywhere you look there are rocks—red rocks, blue rocks, gray rocks, tan rocks, rocks with fossils, volcanic rocks. It is hard to walk here and not experience the desire to bring a sample home; to slip that special piece of earth in your pocket. Consider this one more version of a treasure hunt in the state that is famed for treasure. A rock collection is like a

photo album, a collection of post cards, and a bag full of brochures, but these three dimensional souvenirs can decorate a mantle, garden or dresser.

The first rule for collecting is to look for rocks that you like. They do not need to be worth a lot of money or have exotic mineral structures. If they have a larger story, that is fine, but that comes later when we have a chance to look at mineral books and visit mineral and rock collections at museums and rock shops.

The important thing about rock collecting is the time spent outside looking closely at the land around you.

There are rock shops all over Arizona and they are fun to visit because they are like small museums. If you go into these shops you might find that their staff can impart knowledge about the local area and suggest places you can look for your own specimens. Then as a thank-you to the shop and to prime the child's interest you might buy a small rock to add to the child's collection. Be sure to label where this rock came from just like those you will collect.

You need to prepare for your rock hunting like any prospector. Research the area you want to explore, bring a day pack, a hammer, snacks, sun lotion, insect repellent, a brimmed hat, and lots of water. Note that not all places are open to collecting. For instance, national parks like Petrified Forest feature rocks, but they do not allow collecting. However there are many great places to collect in the National Forests, and on Bureau of Land Management (BLM) land, in mine dumps (where allowed), and on other public lands. Just check first to make sure you and your grandchild are welcome. The BLM booklet *Rockhounding in Arizona* serves as a useful guide.

Round Mountain Rockhound Area, near Safford, has a rough road beyond the registry station and offers some high quality collectibles, including the fire agate! Also look for the jet black Apache Tears, jasper and onyx.

Bonding and bridging:

Here are two more tips: (1) In this dry climate it is hard to predict when it will rain and you might wonder what rain has to do with rock collecting; nevertheless, if you collect after a rain (or bring a spray bottle) you will find that when rocks are wet, it's easier to differentiate them (this is especially true for agates and Apache Tears).

(2) When a child gets excited about rock collecting they will be excited by displays of rocks. This begins a lesson in geology, but the geology follows the passion for collecting. Tucson hosts the highly acclaimed Tucson Gem and Mineral Show for four days every February and this will show not only beautiful gems, rocks, crystals and fossils, but also the equipment that you might want to purchase for this hobby. In Phoenix, the Arizona Mining and Mineral Museum offers a large display area with rocks of all colors and shapes, and maps that show where the rocks were found in the state.

A word to the wise:

If this is something you really want to make a part of your family experience, you might buy a small day pack or a tackle box from the hardware store (with enough room for all your finds), a squirt bottle of water for cleaning rocks, a small brush (like a toothbrush), a small magnifying glass, and a field guide. Put in tissue to protect the fragile ones!

While rock collecting can be a fun lifelong hobby, in the desert there are extra precautions that need to be taken, since venomous insects and snakes live among the rocks. Always use a stick or another object to turn rocks over. Avoid areas near streams or water, because snakes will often rest there.

Age of grandchild: 5 and up; little ones are close to the ground and excellent at finding treasures

Best season: Spring and fall

Contact: Safford Field Office BLM: 711 14th Avenue, Safford, AZ 85546 • (928) 348-4400 • www.blm.gov/az/st/en/fo/safford_field_office.html

Also check out:

Rock hunting sites: www.rockhounds.com/rockshop/azsites.html

Rock collecting for kids: www.rocksforkids.com/

Celebrating the Salsa Trail

Hot weather, hot peppers and a hot time—who would think an event like Salsafest would be a place where you should bring your grandchildren? But it is. Like many others, we love salsa, but we weren't sure that salsa would be good for kids too. One of our friends has a 2½-year-old who loves salsa, so

don't limit your grandkids' choices to refined sugar and high fructose corn syrup—challenge their taste buds in a fun way.

There is a restaurant tasting and salsa-making contest where you and your tray of chips can embark on a mouth-waking adventure, but this is not all that Salsafest provides for entertainment. The tent in the park is buzzing with salsa events, but all around it is a swirl of sound and excitement. Vendors line the street beside the park and a portable stage is a constant source of live music. We watched children dancing around the flagpole; they danced on the grassy lawn and they clapped with the rhythm. The music can be heard throughout the area so you can sit in the grass, on a chair, or just listen as you wander.

On Friday evening one of the really unique experiences is the "hot air balloon glow" on the main street of town. A line of hot air balloons light their flames, causing Main Street to glow. Compare the hot air balloon to a light bulb—when the flame is turned on it also lights up the colorful fabric. Blinking on and off, colors and designs fill the street, the air, and the town. You can walk around them, take photos and enjoy the unique evening.

On Saturday morning the balloons are once again inflated and they take to the air between the mountain ranges, over the cotton fields and to the entertainment of people of all ages gathered on the local school's athletic fields. This is so casual that you can walk up to the balloons, talk to the handlers, and learn as you watch. And as the ground fills with the large inflated fabric your grandchildren will be filled with anticipation. Then one drifts up and another and another until there is a line of dots floating to the horizon!

For the kids there is the added excitement of a piñata bust. If the balloon takeoff had anticipation, imagine the giggles and squirms as one blindfolded participant after another swings away. When it breaks the scramble is on!

Bonding and bridging:

Yes, Salsafest is about salsa, that wonderful combination of tomatoes, onions, spices and peppers. There is magic in the simple list of ingredients and you can find that out yourself in one of two tasting events. Buy a tray of chips and go into the tent for a variety of flavors. It was obvious in the tastings that some of these kids were not new to the idea of salsa. If your grandchild isn't comfortable with hot sauce, make sure you get mild salsa for them, while you're free to explore the hot and exotic flavors.

On Saturday morning go to the tasting tent and watch the amateur contestants as they grind, blend and test their concoctions while putting in the final special ingredient—their own dedication and compassion. Of course the most natural follow-up for this event is to go home and make your own salsa with your grandchild. There are lots of recipes available at the event to help you in your first attempts.

A word to the wise:

Make sure that you have something to drink because it's often hot outside and consuming salsa will warm you up inside too. But the best way to put out the flames isn't a liquid; it's bread or tortillas! Tortillas do more work than simply taste good; the application of flour in the bread or tortilla absorbs the acids present in salsa and neutralizes the spices in the stomach. It is a remedy worth noting on a weekend like this!

Age of grandchild: All

Best season: September

Contact: Graham County Tourism: 1111 Thatcher Blvd. (Hwy 70), Safford, AZ 85546 • (888) 837-1841 • www.salsatrail.com

Also check out:

My Nana's Best Tasting Salsa Challenge: www.salsachallenge.com

Scottsdale Culinary Festival: www.scottsdaleculinaryfestival.org/

Botanical Gardens

In the sun-drenched landscape of Arizona where the raw energy of the earth is so apparent and the vegetation is thin enough to allow you to observe rock, ridge and valley, a person develops a strong desire to be among plants. The plants that grow here are not cuddly; like the landscape, they are fascinating and a little prickly. So how do you introduce your grandchildren to the love of plants, gardens, natural areas? The best way to start is with a botanical garden and there are many excellent ones to choose from in Arizona.

Boyce Thompson Arboretum is located just outside of Superior and a long way from any metropolitan area. This park brings you out to the copper mining country where the founder made his fortunes. Located on Queen Creek with Picketpost Mountain as its backdrop, you are immediately captivated by the contrast between nature and the oasis that is the Arboretum. To enjoy this site you can choose from a variety of mostly short, easy trails that focus on the desert landscapes of the world. The combined length of the trails is 2 miles. There are lots of benches for rest, observing or listening.

The highlight for grandchildren is the Children's Horticultural Garden, which features colorful signage that depicts desert animals and tells important stories that will capture young, creative minds. They can look for treasure, touch and feel the plants, walk in a maze, play with musical instruments and find animal-shaped rocks and chairs scattered throughout the arboretum.

In the Tucson Botanical Garden there are great displays of home patios and the landscaping that accompanies many homes in the region, but the butterfly garden will engage the grandchildren for the longest time. Free-flying butterflies and the tropical plants they love make this little humid greenhouse a place of inspiration. Like fairies, the butterflies drift and flit, often landing on the people who are watching them.

In Phoenix's Desert Botanical Garden the lesson is Xeric! The term xeric refers to an environment that receives ten inches of rainfall or less annually. Gardens in a xeric landscape feature plants that grow with a minimum of water and it's important to find the beauty in these adaptive plants, which reduce demand on the lowering water tables.

Bonding and bridging:

The founder of the Boyce Thompson Arboretum created this living museum from 1923–1929 "to help instill in humanity an appreciation of plants." That seems like a good theme for all your visits. The other botanical collections all serve a similar purpose. Help them see how much variety there is around them and take in the smells and the colors. Keep in mind that it's much better to cut your visit short than to make a long visit into a bad experience.

We exist because of plants and the oxygen, the food, and the shade they provide, but they inspire us too. How did we learn to appreciate the garden? In Judeo-Christian and Islamic theology we began in a garden. Think about letting your grandchild take home a plant from the garden store and learn how to raise it, just as we learn to care for our pets. A cactus (without lots of sharp spines) might be a good one to start with.

A word to the wise:

Botanical gardens change their displays with the seasons and there are holiday exhibits as well. It is good to check each garden's website, get their newsletters and return often. The children will begin to understand seasons and the adaptations that plants and animals make to the natural calendar. Then these same observation can be transferred to nature.

Age of grandchild: 5 and up

Best season: Spring and Fall

Contact: Boyce Thompson Arboretum: 37615 Hwy 60, Superior, AZ 85273 • (520) 689-2723 • http://arboretum.ag.arizona.edu

Tohono Chul Park: 7366 N Paseo del Norte, Tucson, AZ 85704 • (520) 742-6455 • www.tohonochulpark.org

Tucson Botanical Gardens: 2150 N Alvernon Way, Tucson 85712 • (520) 326-9686 • www.tucsonbotanical.org

Also check out:

Desert Botanical Garden: 1201 N Galvin Parkway, Phoenix 85008 • (480) 941-1225 • www.dbg.org

Rocks, Dinosaurs and History— the Museums

Some topics seem to be found in every Arizona museum: rocks and mining, dinosaurs, the Old West, and American Indians, but these familiar topics shouldn't stop you from exploring these museums. We found the Arizona Museum of Natural History in Mesa to be one of the most exciting, inspiring and interactive museums in the state. Wonderful dinosaur reconstructions with actual fossil bones will amaze you and there's a dinosaur footprint you can com-

pare with the size of your own foot; both are just a small part of the experience. This museum engages all the senses and this adds to the experience.

You can also marvel over the reconstructed animals or the animated replicas of fossils in the exhibit that places them within the rock structures where their bones were really found. There is the fun of the periodic flash flood and its accompanying lightning, but more importantly you can move into the Discovery Room and engage in more hands-on activities. In the archaeological displays there are sounds and even scents that trigger ideas and responses.

The Museum of Northern Arizona in Flagstaff does an excellent job with geology and American Indian history and we would recommend this museum for older children with an interest in these subjects. There are reconstructions of ancient villages and the petroglyphs they left behind.

It's most important for you to find museums that help to build upon the experiences you have shared together. For example, the Arizona State Museum in Tucson has one of the most complete stories of the variety of people who settled the geographic region and it is designed as an amazing book put in exhibit form, but it is a "read and absorb" experience which does not fit for all children.

On the other hand the Tucson State History Museum has a wonderful upstairs section that encourages the children to touch, experience and explore. For younger children, this is where the learning takes place. Kids love things they can touch and the newer museum exhibits provide this, but some museums are geared toward adults, and that is okay too. Just make sure you find the museums that will most inspire and teach your grandchild (and you)!

Bonding and bridging:

This continent was settled by a variety of peoples including the English, Irish, French, Spanish, Italian and Germans, and was already inhabited by American Indians prior to settlement. To see an example of this diversity, walk through the wonderful displays of the Arizona State Museum on the University campus in Tucson.

These displays introduce you to many different cultures, each with their own language, stories and lifestyles. The displays also demonstrate how much we have gained by learning from world cultures, and they emphasize how it's impossible to lump every group into a single category. We benefit from the foods, medicines and technology that have been shared by many cultures, and we must be careful when judging and must realize that all cultures have important knowledge to share.

A word to the wise:

These museums can be an exercise in overload. There is so much information that it can be overwhelming, even if we are really interested. Imagine what it is like for little ones who want to climb, touch and be active. On a hot afternoon, an interactive museum like the Tucson History Museum can be great, but the Arizona State Museum is best for children old enough to appreciate the story of the indigenous nations.

Age of grandchild: 5 and up

Best season: When it is too hot to be outside

Contact: Arizona Museum of Natural History: 53 N Macdonald Street, Mesa, AZ 85201 • (480) 644-2230 • www.azmnh.org

Arizona History Museum: 949 E 2nd Street, Tucson, AZ 85719 • (520) 628-5774; www.arizonahistoricalsociety.org

Arizona State Museum, University of Arizona: 1013 E University Blvd., Tucson, AZ 85721-0026 • (520) 621-6302 • www.statemuseum.arizona.edu

Also check out:

Museum of North Arizona, Flagstaff: www.musnaz.org

A child needs a grandparent, anybody's grandparent, to grow a little more securely into an unfamiliar world. CHARLES AND ANN MORSE

River Rafting

In a state not known for its water resources, rivers are the one visible reminder of this life-giving resource. There are 36 rivers in the state, many of which are branches or tributaries of the 10 main rivers. (Mountain streams are often identified as rivers, as well.) The Colorado, Gila, Salt and Verde are the biggest and best-known rivers in Arizona. Because of the exponential growth in

population during the twentieth century, much of Arizona's river water has been diverted for other uses, with a loss of as much as 35% of the perennial flow. On the four biggest rivers (mentioned above), there has been a 91% decrease in free-flowing perennial miles.

People have always been attracted to bodies of water, and many communities have sprung up alongside them. In early history, rivers and lakes were a matter of survival, but as communities expanded over time and moved further away from water sources and water was piped into our homes, rivers and their importance have faded into the background. Sadly, too many rivers became repositories for our wastes, waterborne and otherwise. But times are changing and as the availability of fresh water becomes more critical, individuals and communities are looking at rivers with new eyes. They are becoming places people want to savor and enjoy and river rafting is one such river-based activity that can be relaxing and educational. It is a great way to spend a few hours with a grandchild.

There are many different rafting companies to choose from and in different parts of the state. We spent a lazy afternoon in November on a flatwater trip on the Salt River, named "Rio Salido" by the Spanish and Jesuit explorers because of the presence of salt in its water, which was easily seen when the water was low. Prior to settlement, the rivers were not dammed, and there was a seasonal flow that saw levels rise and fall throughout the year.

Later, we chose to take a four-hour-long float with the Desert Voyagers company. Each inflatable raft could hold one guide and up to eight passengers. Or if there are just two of you, you could choose a Funyak (an inflatable kayak) and follow behind the raft. The trip takes you through the Tonto National Forest with classic Sonoran Desert scenery. Wildlife abounds on the banks, but the wild horses are the most thrilling. They are often found grazing and wading in the water. They are used to paddlers going past and stand peacefully as cameras click.

Bonding and bridging:

Did you read *Tom Sawyer* or *Huckleberry Finn* when you were a child? Did you daydream about setting off on a raft and just letting it carry you downstream to adventures and new places? Your grandchild may not have read either of these classics, but they're good books to read together and then make plans for your own river adventure. You might also think about signing up for a river cleanup together. Most of the major rivers in the state have a special day designed just for this. It is a way of showing your grandchild that you believe in giving back to the rivers, as well as using them; plus you get to spend a day outdoors together. You might choose to visit the new Nina Mason Pulliam Rio Salado Audubon Center, located just a couple miles from downtown Phoenix. Here you can enjoy hiking trails, as well as interactive displays about the river and the restoration of its riparian habitat. Any of these activities could be a prelude or a follow-up to your river excursion.

A word to the wise:

There are two types of rafting to choose from—flatwater and whitewater. Flatwater is probably the best choice for your first excursion and for grand-children under the age of 10. It is also the less expensive of the two. But if you have a grandchild who has rafted before or is a teenager, then a whitewater raft trip may be more fun. For the flatwater trip, realize that younger grandkids may become bored after a time, as the boat slowly floats downstream and the scenery doesn't change dramatically. If at all possible, engage them in paddling or some other task. Be sure to bring along water or other beverages and slather on the sunscreen, since being on water increases the chance of sunburn.

Age of grandchild: 5 years to teenager

Best season: Daily, year-round—two trip times offered each day

Contact: 2505 N Brimhall, Mesa, AZ 85203 • (480) 998-7238 • www.desertvoyagers.com

Also check out:

www.inaraft.com

www.blackcanyonadventures.com

www.saltrivertubing.com

Arizona Museum for Youth

The name of this museum does not give you any clue that it is a treasure waiting to be discovered by you and your grandchild. When you walk through the doors you enter a space that focuses completely on interactive exhibits and the visual arts. There are many great children's museums in existence that include art in some manner, but a museum focused strictly on art is unique.

Children are natural-born artists. They have no natural limitations on how they present what they perceive or what their imaginations suggest. It is only as we grow older that we become critical of our artistic abilities. I remember all too well my mortification in first grade when I incorrectly cut a robin out

of construction paper. Somehow I just didn't understand the directions and I felt humiliated. I managed to enjoy creating art through the rest of my school years, but the experience of "doing it wrong" stayed with me, and that's one thing young children should never feel about this form of expression.

This museum has two sections—the largest area is called the Gallery Space and it is divided into two areas. The ArtZone is a wonderful space with many different hands-on activity stations that explore art processes using line, color and textures. The other half is exhibit space, with exhibits changing throughout the year. In the ArtZone there are lots of tables with chairs around them, where you and your grandchild can try your hand at Japanese Sumi-E (ink and wash painting) or Gyotaku (fish rubbings), or use crayons and plastic stencil shapes.

Just across the hall from the ArtZone is another smaller room called the Family Zone. This is set up for families to eat snacks, rest with very little ones, or just have a space to relax together with books.

On the opposite side of the building is ArtVille which is designed for younger children (0-4). There is room for lots of imaginary play including things to climb on and slides to go down. A child-sized series of rooms includes a playhouse with kids books on the walls of the "living room," and a full kitchen set up with lots of play food items.

Bonding and bridging:

Before humans had a written language, we had art. People told their stories on cave walls and cliffs, or through etchings on rocks. As we became "civilized," written words became the main form of transferring important information, but our brains have not changed so much over all the centuries and art still expresses what we hold in our hearts and minds.

From the time your grandchildren are toddlers, keep crayons and scrap paper handy. Even a two-year-old enjoys seeing what happens as they move a crayon across paper. When they are three, they are ready for coloring books, although staying within the lines may be difficult. Small scissors are just right for four- or five-year-olds. Keep old magazines for cutting practice and have some glue sticks handy too. With very little material, your grandkids can spend hours creating "art." Then make a special wall where you hang their creations, so they will see their work prominently displayed.

A word to the wise:

As with all museums, too much of a good thing can become tedious, so always leave while the kids are still enthusiastic about the experience and want to return. Plan your visits so that each visit there will be something new to see or try. The Museum has plans for future expansion and we hope they come true. It is a great place as is, but it could become so much more. Be sure to call in advance to make sure there are no closures due to construction. Also check ahead for seasonally related special events and the Meet the Artist program for the temporary exhibitions.

Age of grandchild: Toddler–12

Best season: All

Contact: 35 N Robson Street, Mesa, AZ 85201 • (480) 644-2467 • www.arizonamuseumforyouth.com

Also check out:

Tucson Children's Museum: www.tucsonchildrensmuseum.org

Children's Museum of Phoenix: www.childrensmuseumofphoenix.org

If you don't know [your family's] history, then you don't know anything. You are a leaf that doesn't know it is part of a tree. Michael Crichton

Arizona Science Center

The stated mission of the Arizona Science Center is "to inspire, educate and entertain people of all ages," and we would have to say they accomplish all three goals. Located in the Science and Heritage Square in downtown Phoenix, this massive, concrete monolith of a building is not especially inspiring, but the three floors of interactive exhibits are.

This Science Center is best suited for children who are able to read, because all of the interactive exhibits (over 300) require reading skills so the child can know how to operate the exhibits or to understand their purpose. Children who can't read tend to just run from one exhibit to the other pushing buttons and waiting for something to happen.

There are three floors to the Center and each one has a couple of galleries with enough exhibits and information to occupy a person for a good hour or more. On the first floor you'll find the "All About You Gallery," which focuses on the human body and how it works, as well as the "Psychology Gallery," which covers areas of memory, perceptions and why we act the way we do. The second floor features the "Magnetism and Electricity Gallery" where you'll find activities that cover physics and electricity. Going up to the 3rd floor you pass a room designed to look at music and sound—it is small, but full of fascinating inventions.

On the 3rd floor there is also a room that focuses on the earth's atmosphere and geology and here is one exhibit your grandkids (and you) will really remember. It's called Forces of Nature. You stand on a platform about the size of a boxing ring with TV screens up above that show a video of extreme weather or acts of God, such as earthquakes and forest fires. In each example you feel some of the effects—wind blowing, water spraying, the ground beneath shaking, hot lights above; the grandkids will love the experience and you will smile at their enjoyment, while secretly enjoying it yourself. Don't be surprised if they want to go back and do it again.

The last gallery—My Digital World—is one the grandkids will probably understand and enjoy much more than you. But here they may have the chance to teach you something (or at least try to teach you). Internet technology is the future that seems to have leapt upon us overnight and will be the future our grandchildren live with. Maybe all we can do is stand back and shake our heads in confused awe.

Bonding and bridging:

The Science Center provides grandparents and grand-children with the opportunity to learn new things together. For example, in the Psychology Gallery one exhibit asks us to think about how we read people's emotions by their facial expressions. These are photographs of actual people's faces that can be turned to show the mouth, or the eyes, or the forehead in different expressions. Try it on one another— see if they can read your expression and you can read theirs.

So many interactive exhibits can lead to overstimulation in younger children and "meltdowns" when it's time to leave. Even for older kids, there is a point where they (and we) reach supersaturation. It might be best to either set a time limit or choose one or two galleries to focus on and plan to come back another time to see the others. It's always better to quit while everyone is still enjoying themselves than when we're overloaded and worn out.

A word to the wise:

While this museum has more than enough activities to engage your grand-child for hours, there are several activities that will attract their attention which require an extra fee—the SkyCycle, the Climbing Wall, IMAX, Planetarium, and special exhibits. Decide beforehand if you're willing to spend for extras (and how much) and let the kids know before entering so everyone will be "on the same page" and leave happy to have had the experience. Additionally, Science Saturdays are a special opportunity for you to share with grandchildren aged 6–10; you'll learn about a variety of topics in hands-on sessions with Science Center staff in a classroom setting.

Age of grandchild: 5 and older

Best season: Any

Contact: 600 E Washington Street, Phoenix, AZ 85004-2394 • (602) 716-2000 • www.azscience.org

Also check out:

Arizona Mining and Mineral Museum: www.admmr.state.az.us/general/museum.html

Bisbee Mining and Historical Museum: www.bisbeemuseum.org

Children's Museum of Phoenix

From the outside it is obvious that this grand, classical building was once a school. The historic Monroe School was built in 1913, but closed in 1972. Converting it to a museum required extensive renovations, but the renovations were a success and today the museum's mission is "to engage the minds, muscles and imaginations of children today." The museum combines color, design and educational content into one of the most child-friendly places possible.

The wide stairways and hallways of this three story building may cause some grandparents to flashback to their days in elementary school. In fact, the Museum is asking alumni to send in photos, memories or newspaper clippings that show what it was like to attend school here. The goal is to have a multigenerational treasure hunt throughout the Museum, where grandparents and their grandkids can look back in time, as well as to the future.

Like many Children's Museums there is a Marketplace. This one has lots of shelves with a variety of pretend food items, both "fresh" and packaged. There are cash registers for those who want to be "workers" and grocery carts for those who want to play the role of mom or dad. One very popular table is filled with dried split peas that the kids can scoop up and weigh. Next to this is the Texture Cafe—where the child can be customer or cook and there are lots of little stoves and sinks and "food" to prepare. Think about the way children try to emulate adults. Here they encounter adult settings but are not told how to fulfill the roles they choose. Whether it is a market, or a clinic—the story is theirs to create. Next to the kitchen is a room with a variety of tubes and tracks to roll balls and watch their progress. This is a place, according to the staff, where older kids choose to spend lots of time.

There are too many fun exhibits and activities to list here, but the important thing to remember is that the grandparent's job is to guide children through the museum, letting the child's imagination make the choices, while you watch over safety and the possible conflict that can arise from lots of little hands and feet concentrating on the objects that have grabbed their attention and not on who else is grabbing, where people are walking, and who is crawling nearby.

Bonding and bridging:

This museum really incorporates art well into the exhibits. This seems a fitting tribute to Jackson Pollock, one of Monroe's alumni. Much of the art was previously used, and it has been reused to make pretty, playful or even strange art objects, like the entire wall glittering with hundreds of CDs that have been suspended from the ceiling just past the admissions area. In the play kitchen area on the 2nd floor, look up above and you will see silverware art—lots of forks, knives, and spoons welded together and hanging from the ceiling. Some are easily recognizable shapes like birds and other animals, while others require more imagination. After looking at the museum's artwork, go to the Art Studio where there are tables covered with newspaper and a variety of materials for making art. Museum staff are on hand to help, and each week there are 2–3 different projects to work on. You can create together or just be part of the audience.

A word to the wise:

It's easy for kids and grandparents alike to end up exhausted after walking up and down the stairs (there are elevators too) and walking from one exhibit and activity to the next. Before anyone gets too worn out, take advantage of the Museum's Book Loft—a space that encourages everyone to slow down, relax and enjoy some quiet reading, whether you are reading to them, or they are reading to you. There are formal story times scheduled each day. Reading to our grandchildren is something that helps us build strong and long-lasting bonds, plus it is another way to instill a love of literature and the lifelong joy of reading books.

Age of grandchild: Infant–10

Best season: All

Contact: 215 N 7th Street, Phoenix, AZ 85034 • (602) 253-0501 • www.childrensmuseumofphoenix.org

Also check out:

Tucson Children's Museum: www.tucsonchildrensmuseum.org

Arizona Museum of Youth: www.arizonamuseumforyouth.com

Even now, I am not old. I never think of it, and yet I am a grandmother to eleven grandchildren. GRANDMA MOSES

Hall of Flame Fire Museum

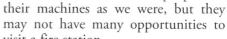

All of us grandparents who grew up in urban areas remember the large brick or stone firehouse (also known as the fire station) that was found in almost every neighborhood. At some point in our early years, we probably had a chance to visit the firehouse and meet the firemen who lived and worked there. Policemen and firemen have always inspired awe in children. Firefighters, however, have an additional aura because of their shiny, flashy, red firetrucks. Children today are in just as much in awe of these people and their machines as we were, but they may not have many opportunities to visit a fire station.

The Hall of Flame Fire Museum is both a historical museum and a place for educating youth. Located near Papago Park, the museum is based on the collection of one individual who originally displayed his collection in Wisconsin. Now the collection has grown to six exhibit galleries with over 130 vehicles that date from push carts and horse-drawn carriages all the way up to the modern era. Each is displayed so you can see it from all angles, and enjoy the color, the design, and the growing sophistication of fire fighting technology. The bright colors are a natural draw for children who might not appreciate all the strange variations that will entertain the grandparents.

The museum is also a hall of heroes and the museum recognizes the valor of all firefighters—from those serving small towns to those who lost their lives in the tragedy of the Twin Towers. Your children can learn about real heroes (in contrast to those they cheer for on a sports field). Imagine how hard it is for them to understand how someone would risk their lives for strangers! Help them understand heroism and valor.

While grandparents admire the antique engines and other equipment, the kids can explore the hands-on section of the museum and learn about fire safety. The children's section includes a play area with lots of physical activity, as well as jigsaw puzzles and a mini-theater. Finally there is the Wildland Fire Fighting exhibit that reminds us that the danger of fire is not limited to our homes, and that people are responsible for starting many wildfires as well as protecting our communities from their damage. This is another complicated lesson because wildfires can be good for the natural landscape too.

Bonding and bridging:

Our grandchildren's safety is foremost in all our minds and whenever we can do something to help them stay safe, the better we feel. We want to teach them to be aware of dangers that exist without creating irrational fears. We know that fire is something children find enticing. They're drawn to it just like moths are to flames and we want them to think of fire as something to be enjoyed around a campfire or in a fireplace, with adults present. In a museum such as this one, we can combine that sort of education and cautionary lessons in ways that are both fun and practical. Demonstrate a drop and roll for the kids and they will be tickled and want to try it. You might involve their parents too in a discussion about planned escape routes in their home, in case of fire. Most of us never do this, preferring to believe that such a crisis will never occur.

A word to the wise:

Many household fires are started unintentionally by children playing with matches, so a little knowledge is good for everyone. Teach your grandchild the difference as you light campfires, also teach them how to put fires out. As you light your grills, show them how to do it safely and what to do when you are done. You have many opportunities to let them learn in your everyday life and a visit like this can provide the basis for such learning.

Age of grandchild: 4–10

Best season: All

Contact: 6101 East Van Buren Street, Phoenix, AZ 85008-3421 • (602) 275-3473 • www.halloflame.org

Also check out:

Phoenix Police Museum: www.phoenixpolicemuseum.com

Tombstone historic fire department: http://tps.cr.nps.gov/nhl/detail.cfm?ResourceId=88&ResourceType=District

Four historic fire towers at Grand Canyon: www.nps.gov/grca/naturescience/cynsk-v13.htm

My grandkids believe I'm the oldest thing in the world.
And after two or three hours with them, I believe it, too. GENE PERRET

The Heard Museum

The Heard is a long-standing institution in the city of Phoenix. It is a living museum with a unique combination of art, history and culture and a specific focus and emphasis on the American Indians of the Southwest. The beautiful building is in the white adobe style and opened in 1929 shortly after the death of Dwight Heard. His widow Maie acted as director, curator and guide for the next 20 years. Since then the Museum has grown in size, although the beautiful southwestern architecture remains.

You may have taken your grandchild to other art museums, but this one is special because it focuses solely on the cultures of the American Indians and the beauty of the art they have created over the centuries. Art defines people's view of the world and one way to come to know a people is by seeing their art. Nevertheless, one of the challenges with visiting any museum with children is the hands-off nature of the experience. While all people enjoy looking at beautiful creations, our hands, especially those of little ones, itch to touch, and at the Heard there are opportunities for just that.

There are 10 galleries in the Museum, but some will hold more fascination for your grandchildren than others. "We Are!" is an exhibit that focuses on the 21 federally recognized tribal communities in the state. This is where you will find many of the hands-on activities kids enjoy, as well as personal accounts of what life is like today for Native people. Here you can try weaving on a loom, or making paper flowers in the style of the Yaqui. In the gallery "Every Picture Tells A Story" you and your grandchild can take a tour around the US and see how local wildlife and vegetation have inspired American Indian art. This exhibit also includes hands-on opportunities to create art. Finally, for the older grandchild, you may want to visit "Remembering Our Indian School Days: The Boarding School Experience," which tells the story of four generations through personal mementos, photos and written accounts of Native Americans. It's not necessarily a happy story, but one that every generation of Americans should know about.

Bonding and bridging:

A museum like this gives your grandchild the opportunity to see and learn about the diverse cultures that existed in the area before European settlement. It also gives you a chance to talk about your heritage. The history of the settlement of the US is not an especially happy or easy issue to discuss, but our grandchildren will grow up in a complex world where all nations are closely tied by economics, politics, religion and sports, and learning to respect and understand other cultures will be critical to their future. What better place to begin that process than right here in our own state. Another fun way to meet people of other backgrounds and cultures is to attend one of the festivals hosted by the Heard throughout the year. Live performers and artists will engage them and the opportunity to create their own works of art will make the museum experience feel that much more real.

A word to the wise:

As with all visits to museums (other than children's museums) everyone can become overwhelmed or saturated quite quickly when you're just walking and looking, so decide ahead of time to visit just a few of the galleries or one that your grandchild considers a favorite and maybe add one more to each visit. Bring along a tablet and some crayons or colored pencils and encourage them to pick out a piece of art that they especially like and try to capture it on paper.

Age of grandchild: 8 and older

Best season: All seasons

Contact: 2301 N Central Avenue, Phoenix, AZ 85004 • (602) 252-8848 • www.heard.org

Also check out:

The Amerind Foundation, Dragoon, AZ: www.amerind.org

Gold Fever

No other state has a more exciting set of legends and ghost towns tied to a compulsion for gold. Our grandchildren have grown up with the adventures of treasure seekers like Indiana Jones and Captain Jack Sparrow, so it should be easy to interest them in the stories of real-life gold-seekers of the past.

Nothing compares with the Lost Dutchman Mine, a legendary gold mine that is memorialized in a State Park near Apache Junction and carries the mine's name. Hiking trails lead up to Superstition Mountain and the landscape that surrounds your adventure is filled with desert ecology and impressive geology.

Maybe a viewing of the old Glenn Ford movie *Lust for Gold* would be good to watch first, or you could visit the Goldfield ghost town that is now more of an Old West entertainment and souvenir site to get your grandchildren excited. Then, of course, there are books with stories about the legendary Lost Dutchman mine.

More than anything, gold fever is great motivation for a hike. You can join the legions of other trekkers and get good exercise and exploration in the process. There may be "gold in them thar hills," but if you have a wonderful outdoor experience with your grandchildren you will have uncovered grandparent gold. Some seasons will have birds flitting around; sometimes after the rare rains there will be desert blooms. You can remind your grandchildren that this area was a different kind of treasure chest to the Apaches and other tribes who lived here, before gold was discovered. They found that life in the desert provided them with the real rewards of food, water and shelter.

Not all gold miners failed. The Vulture Mine near Wickenburg made Henry Wickenburg temporarily famous and wealthy and the town of Wickenburg is a contrast to the abandoned ghost settlement of this site. Today it is privately owned and you must pay a fee, but this is where you can show your grandchild the remains of a successful venture. What you see today was also the site of Vulture City, which had a population of 5,000 in its heyday. Can you imagine that today? This is what you want to explore with your grandchild, not just what you can see, but the history that helped create what you see.

Bonding and bridging:

Greed is not a topic we normally discuss with grand-kids, but it is worth talking about as you complete these visits. Greed is one of humanity's darker qualities, but every generation must deal with it and its consequences. One of the more graphic reminders of greed at the Vulture Mine is a tree. It is gnarled and ragged, evidence of life in a harsh environment. It became the Hanging Tree for at least 18 men who could not resist stealing the gold they were hired to mine and process.

Ask your grandchild what they think is valuable. See if they understand how your love for them has more value than anything they could give you. Money is good for some things, but money is not the only measure of wealth. That is a concept that cannot be emphasized enough if you want to give them every opportunity for success and happiness.

A word to the wise:

These locations are exposed to the sun's heat and there is little water, so you must protect yourself, but there are other hazards too. In the summer there are rattlesnakes and scorpions that you need to be aware of. Animals and cactus spines aren't the biggest hazard, however. There is broken glass, uneven terrain, and potentially dangerous old metal and other trash, all of which are part of the old story. You need not scare your grandchildren, but you will want to make sure you keep them focused on some of the dangers so that the time you share is positive in every way.

Age of grandchild: 8 and up

Best season: Avoid the heat of midsummer

Contact: Vulture Mine: 55402 N Vulture Mine Road, Wickenburg, AZ 85390 • (602) 859-2743 • www.jpc-training.com/vulture.htm

Lost Dutchman State Park: 6109 N Apache Trail, Apache Junction, AZ 85219 • (480) 982-4485 • www.stateparks.com/lost_dutchman.html

Also check out:

Superstition Mountain Museum: 4087 N Apache Trail, Apache Junction, AZ 85219: (480) 983-4888 • Adds to the story of the Lost Dutchman Mine • www.superstitionmountainmuseum.org

When grandparents enter the door, discipline flies out the window. OGDEN NASH

Arcosanti

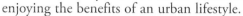

Arcosanti is as exotic as it sounds. Just three miles from busy Interstate 17, near Prescott, it can't be seen until you drive down a curving dirt road. There, spread out in the desert, are the concrete structures that make up this futuristic and idealistic community. This is the dream of Paolo Soleri, an Italian architect who studied under Frank Lloyd Wright. Arcology (a combination of the words architecture and ecology) is the name he gave to the concept of a new way for people to live in harmony with the earth, while still enjoying the benefits of an urban lifestyle.

Arcosanti is the manifestation of this concept, combining community, art, functional design and self-sufficiency. Construction on the site has been going on since 1970, so you will see both completed buildings, and others that are still under construction. Funding issues have resulted in slow progress, but the project continues to draw students and volunteers.

This is a place to bring an older grandchild, especially one who has shown an interest in architecture, engineering or the environmental movement, because all three components are present in this unique experiment in living. Tours are given every day on the hour and even though the visitor is welcome to wander the grounds and trails on their own, a tour is the best way to learn what life is like for those who have chosen to live here.

Paolo Soleri, now in his 90s, still comes to Arcosanti once a week and holds an informal gathering with students, staff and visitors to discuss current projects, philosophy, and any other questions students or workers may have. He is a frail, small man, with a halo of white hair and hearing loss, but a mind that still is filled with ideas and enthusiasm for the future. These are one-hour-long sessions and worth attending; call ahead to see if he will be there.

The other important component of Arcosanti is the production of the Soleri Windbells. These are bronze wind chimes, all designed by Soleri. They are the major source of income for the site. There is a special open-air studio where the bronze is heated to 2200°F and poured into the molds. The heat used in this process is reused by channeling it into the floor in the winter months. There is a store in the main building that sells these wind chimes, which come in all sizes and prices. More than a souvenir, these chimes are works of art.

Bonding and bridging:

If you are a baby boomer, your grandchildren will eventually ask if you were a hippie or lived in a commune. Whether you did or not, you no doubt have memories of that era, which was tumultuous with change. Just like other generations, we were seeking new ways of doing things and rebelling against the institutions and ideas of our elders. We have already gone through this period with our own children, and now as grandparents, we hopefully have more patience and wisdom to accept and understand the struggles our grandchildren face as they grow into young adults. This is a good place to talk about dreams, about having the vision to create something totally new, even as others challenge or discourage you. Paolo Soleri was a dreamer. Was he successful? Will his dream survive? This is the time to let our grandchildren know that they can pursue whatever their dreams might be, and to keep heart when they come up against obstacles.

A word to the wise:

There are a lot of steps to go up and down on the grounds and on the tour, and since people do live here, be sure your grandchild knows to not wander off. It is possible to stay overnight at Arcosanti, which gives you more time to explore the 4,000-acre preserve, but be aware that the lodging is comparable to a European hostel—clean, but quite spartan. There is a café in the main building where you can buy meals.

Age of grandchild: 12 or older

Best season: Any

Contact: Interstate 17 Exit 262 at Cordes Junction—3 miles north and east from junction • HC 74, Box 4136, Mayer, AZ 86333 • (928) 632-7135 • www.arcosanti.org

Also check out:

Biosphere 2: www.b2science.org

Cosanti, Paradise Valley: (480) 948-6145; (800) 752-3187 • www.cosanti.com

How beautifully the leaves grow old. How full of light and color are their last days. John Burroughs

77

Ancient Settlements: Exploring the Mysteries of the Past

When we look to trace our personal family history we go to libraries and genealogical resources so that we can provide future generations with a sense of their roots. Arizona provides us with unusually rich resources to help us to see what historical North America was like: the world that Coronado found when he was looking for the lost cities of gold, the world that preceded all European exploration and "discovery."

Take them to see Casa Grande (Hokokam) where a giant four-story building rises above the creosote bush desert and is shaded by a structure that diverts rain and erosion. Or explore Montezuma Castle (a very misleading name) to find a magnificent Sinagua village perched within the recesses of a cliff. Or hire a guide to take you to the Puebloan ruins of Canyon de Chelly. Or visit Wupatki, to see the "high-rise" apartments. At sites like these you can help your grandchildren connect with the roots of the continent.

Think of the richness of the names as you introduce your grandchildren to the Anasazi (Pueblo Indians), the Hohokam, the Sinagua, and the mountain Mogollon—the Paleo-Indian pioneers. The Dine (Navajo), Paiute, Apache and others are their descendants.

When you visit these sites, the architecture is only part of the story. What was everyday life like here? What about the games that they played? Here are ball courts like you will find in Mexico and southern Arizona. Games were as much a part of ancient community life as they are today, but in a much different way. No scores, no newspapers. Yet the game was obviously significant when you consider the work it must have taken to create the courts!

At Montezuma Castle you can talk about safety and how hard it would have been to get up and down the ladders between buildings and from the ground. At Casa Grande you can discuss the need for water and all the irrigation work that would be required to live in such an environment. When would the people who lived here take baths or showers? How much water does your grandchild use in a day compared to the families that lived here? Visit Montezuma Well and look at the limestone sink with all the water that would have been available here. How does it compare to the other sites? Which of the places would they want to live at?

Bonding and bridging:

These are adventures for the young if you prepare them for the exploration of early civilizations. Connect them with their own family tree and why it is so important that they learn who their own ancestors are and where they came from. Share what you know about people and places in your own history, how the people traveled from far locations to come together and produce your family and what it has meant to each generation.

Then challenge them to join you on an exploration of the history of people who have disappeared in the flow of time. These are the ancestors to modern Indian nations, the people who first learned how to live in the desert. What can you learn from them? How does their ability to adjust to the challenges of the environment relate to our civilization and the challenges we face with water, climate and resources?

A word to the wise:

Grandchildren can become bored with one "ruin" after another. Take these a day at a time, with food and play interspersed. Compare where you stay and what you eat with what the children who grew up at each location would have experienced. Children respond to other children and that is where you can build their interest and curiosity.

Age of grandchild: All

Best season: Fall, winter and spring, when it is cooler

Contact: Montezuma Castle National Monument: PO Box 219, Campe Verde, AZ 86322 • (928) 567-3322 • www.nps.gov/moca

Tuzigoot National Monument: PO Box 219, Campe Verde, AZ 86322 • www.nps.gov/tuzi/index.htm • (928) 634-5564

Wupatki National Monument: 6400 N Highway 89, Flagstaff, AZ 86004 • (928) 679-2365 • www.nps.gov/wupa

Casa Grande Ruins National Monument: 1100 W Ruins Drive, Coolidge, AZ 85128 • (520) 723-3172 • www.nps.gov/cagr

Also check out:

Navajo National Monument: www.nps.gov/nava

Sedona: Finding A Vortex

Sedona has a reputation as one of the most beautiful locations in Arizona, but there are many other places that might serve as competition. The New Age movement values Sedona for an even more important reason, as they consider it to be one of the unique places on earth where there is a phenomenon called a vortex. It is during the grandparent's generation that

the word and the phenomenon began to attract interest. A vortex is described as a place of energy, but the exact definition isn't important. In short, a vortex is a place where there seems to be a special harmony with nature. It is a place that gives us a special satisfaction or inspiration. Why is that? Can you explore that idea with your grandchildren? What do they like here? Does the color of the rock make any difference? Would it be as nice if the rock was brown or black or gray? Use your camera to capture the images of the landscape. Ask your grandchild to take photos of all the things they find special. The reason to engage in this adventure with your grandchildren is to explore special places, not to determine whether vortexes really exist.

Boynton Canyon is the most remote vortex and requires the most hiking, so this would be appropriate for middle school-aged children. Cathedral Rock can be seen from many places and the stream you cross can help you cool off and be a chance to play, while Bell Rock and Airport Mesa are mostly drive-by sites, with a small walk to discover what they offer.

Red Rock State Park has a visitor center that provides an excellent set of interpretive displays to help you and your grandchildren understand the natural world that surrounds this outstanding display of red rocks. It will help you see the contrast between the forests, the dry desert plants and the unique biology of the riparian area along the stream and the life within the waters. This is an important place to get grounded amongst the talk of vortexes. Naturalist programs cover geology, astronomy, bird life, and history. Sunset and moonlight hikes will give your family a very different perspective of the area.

If it is true that these places calm us, that they inspire us we can use them to discover ourselves as well. Walking in any of these places with your grandchildren is an opportunity to see the colors of the landscape, take in the sounds of wind and water, observe birds and get good exercise.

Bonding and bridging:

Each of the places mentioned here provide places to sit and contemplate. Kids are not used to this kind of experience, so a digital camera, or a tablet with colored pencils or crayons can be as important as the water and snacks that you bring for energy.

Is there a place where you feel inspired? Does it matter if you go around the next corner or over the next ridge? If you can visit more than one of these places, you can compare them. You can talk about what they have in common or why one place feels better to you than another. That is what the original people who created the vortex maps did.

When we were here, people played flutes, enjoyed picnics, waded in the streams, while others mountain biked. Each person must find their own way of enjoying the area without detracting from others' enjoyment.

A word to the wise:

If the weather is hot, kids will love Slide Rock State Park where the water moves through natural pathways in the sandstone. Here the kids can wade, splash and float their toys in small, interconnected pools. Natural water chutes make this a natural water park, one that predates all the commercial water attractions in the state. Be aware that in the summer this is one of the most popular destinations in the Oak Canyon area and the park no longer accepts newcomers when the lot is full.

The Park is also an old homestead with an apple orchard and if you are there on the right weekend in September you can participate in an Apple Festival.

Age of grandchild: 8 and up

Best season: All

Contact: Red Rock District, Coconino National Forest: PO Box 20429 Sedona, AZ 86341-0429 • (928) 203-2900 • www.redrockcountry.org

Red Rock State Park: 4050 Red Rock Loop Road, Sedona, AZ 86336 • (928) 282-6907 • http://azstateparks.com/parks/rero

Also check out:

Red Rock Scenic Byway: www.redrockscenicbyway.com

If a child is to keep alive his inborn sense of wonder, he needs the companionship of at least one adult who can share it, rediscovering with him the joy, excitement and mystery of the world we live in. Rachel Carson

Jeep Rides

In reading this book, you will notice that we are not big promoters of motorized recreation. Instead, we encourage others to enjoy using their own bodies and energy to explore the world and that definitely applies to our grandchildren. However, we know there are grandparents who are not physically able to hike or do some of the other activities we recommend, and a jeep tour is one way to explore the backcountry with your grandchildren. We also found

many people recommending that we go for a jeep ride in the Sedona area. They told us that it was not only fun for the grandkids, but for them too. Many of us grandparents have fond memories of seeing Roy Rogers and Dale Evans bouncing over the western landscape in their trusty jeep; maybe you even had the toy version. So, here we followed the advice of others and our own nostalgia and signed up for a Pink Jeep Tour.

There are any number of jeep tour companies in Sedona, but we arbitrarily chose the Pink version, because they are the original jeep tour company and their jeeps just looked fun. A granddaughter might choose this company because of its Barbie jeep colors. We were also pleased to learn that our tour would take us on pre-established, permitted routes within the National Forest land. One concern we have always had with off-roading and 4x4 adventures is the damage that can be done by vehicles to fragile desert landscapes, but these jeeps stay on long-used rutted trails. Each jeep has a highly trained driver/guide (certified by the National Association for Interpretation) who will explain some of the area's history—both natural and human—to you and your fellow passengers. There are a number of options for tours, some as short as 1½ hours and others as long as 4 hours. The destination of the tour also determines the level of adventure you will experience in the ride itself. Most kids want the maximum ride, but you can choose what is best for both of you.

There are scheduled stops during the tour when you can get out, stretch your legs, relax your grip, and walk across the ancient rocks that make up this red rock country. There are many other jeep tour companies operating around the state, but few are able to compete with this scenery.

Bonding and bridging:

This is an activity that is worthy of lots of photographs. Not only of the incredible scenery all around you, but of people's expressions in the jeep as it leaps and bounds across the rocks. Take turns taking photos of your grandchild and let them take some of you. Some will no doubt be blurry because of the jouncing vehicle, but others will capture the pure glee and disbelief as you go up and down seemingly impossible grades. The activity is more like an amusement ride and so it is not likely to lend itself to many serious discussions. When the jeeps stop and you have a chance to walk around, try to find a quiet spot and spend a few moments just listening. This will be difficult because there are normally many jeeps stopped together, but if at all possible, try to find the silence that once filled these magnificent canyons. Ask your grandchild if they find this place beautiful and why or why not. Then tell them how you feel in this setting.

A word to the wise:

Because these vehicles bounce up and down, and go around steep curves and up and down lots of rocks, there is always the possibility of someone feeling carsick. If you have a grandchild with this condition, it may not be the best choice of an activity, but if they really want to do it, be sure to take preventive medication well enough in advance that you and they can enjoy the experience. It may be no accident that the jeeps we rode in were the color of Pepto-Bismol. Bring along bottled water, a hat and sunscreen. If it hasn't rained in a while, the trails will be dusty.

Age of grandchild: 5 and up

Best season: Fall, winter and spring

Contact: 204 N State Route 89A, Sedona, AZ 86336 • (800) 873-3662 • www.pinkjeep.com

Also check out:

www.sedonaoffroadadventures.com

www.safarijeeptours.com

www.redrockjeep.com

www.apachetrailtours.com/tours

To our children we give two things: one is roots, the other, wings. ANDY ROONEY

Petrified Forest National Park

We all love beautiful rocks, especially when they have brilliant colors and concentric circles. Some places feature agates, some are known for fossils, but only the Petrified Forest has massive ancient trees that have changed into long, linear agates. Petrified logs decorate the multicolored badlands; trunks of an ancient wet lowland forest are now exposed in a desert landscape!

You should begin your exploration with the museum on the south end of the park to help your grandchild understand the trails and vistas that you are going to explore. On the north end, the Painted Desert is beautiful, but not as engaging for the children who will be more fascinated by trees turned to stone. Find out the rules for where you can walk off the road and make your own discoveries.

The park is designed to capture the historic story of the landforms, the varied people that lived and worked here, as well as the story the fossils tell. Your challenge is to put these stories together so they enrich the day.

Help the children see the actions of time, water and soil represented in the bands of color. Signage helps you understand that this represents an ancient climate and a window into history. We see lizards today, but once there were dinosaurs roaming about. This rich, forested landscape included at least eleven species of trees, over two hundred different species of plants and a diversity of both predators and prey. The Rainbow Forest Museum has reconstructed some of the animals that would have wandered among the giant trees.

There is another type of "sign" altogether at Newspaper Rock. To protect this amazing set of petroglyphs you must view from a platform at the top of the rim. They serve both as art and a signpost from the past.

To see how the early inhabitants also enjoyed the beauty of the logs, visit Agate House, a seven-room ancient pueblo built with petrified wood. Strangely, there are no trees here today, except for the cottonwoods along the streams, so that means that there is no shade and the midday temperatures can be dangerous. Bring not only water, but beverages with electrolytes as well. Wear a hat, use sunscreen and plan ahead.

Bonding and bridging:

How do we know we are seeing trees? How about setting the children up to see for themselves? Find an old tree trunk, but one that is still in the forest, not a fossil. Look at the layers of growth from bark to heartwood. Show them the annual rings and the scar where branches break off from the main trunk. The exciting thing about fossils is that we can apply our knowledge of today's biology and we can recognize traces of today's biology in fossils of the past. The basic form of the tree has not changed, even if species have.

Knowledge involves looking at details and making comparisons, and information is richest when examined in context, and you can be the conduit for knowledge in this park. You can give your grandchildren the gift of science and you can light up their world with the satisfaction of learning. And the best thing is that you can learn too!

A word to the wise:

We hear about overcoming temptation, but where do we learn this difficult concept? When do we get to practice the act of denial? How about starting here? Greedy visitors, profit seekers, and just plain oblivious individuals have taken away more of the Petrified Forest than we can now see. They then let their "souvenirs" collect dust on shelves where they are often forgotten and tossed out. So here is the challenge; we can look, we can touch, but we cannot take it with us. No—not even a little piece. Explain that this is a treasure that belongs to everyone. Tell them that they would not like people to take one of their toys each time they visited their house and we should not take what belongs to everyone from this very special place. It is the beginning of an ethic.

Age of grandchild: 5 and up

Best season: Avoid the summer if you can

Contact: PO Box 2217, Petrified Forest, AZ 86028 • (928) 524-6228 • www.nps.gov/pefo

Also check out:

Museum of Northern Arizona, Flagstaff: www.musnaz.org

Arizona Museum of Natural History, Mesa: www.azmnh.org/

Sunset Crater National Monument

The ground here consists of a variety of lava marbles—rough marble, not the smooth toys we play with. The lava was too filled with gas when it exploded into the air to create solid, smooth balls. Rather, these marbles are a lightweight collection of cinders that roll and clatter over one another. There are also lava flows that moved across the landscape in a hot, viscous mass that froze into syrupy-looking rock formations filled with cavities and thick, ropy formations. In terms of geologic time, Sunset Crater is a recent volcano, as it last erupted

around 1050. It created a landscape that was new and fertile and the Indians at Walnut Canyon just to the south used this new soil for their crops when they created their cliff dwellings around 1100. The elaborate villages of Wupatki National Monument just to the north were also based on the rich new soil that supported the village crops.

As you walk the various trails of the Monument, the land is dominated by the blackness of the cinders and the pastel colors of the sparse vegetation that grows on these piles of stone. At first glance, the area does not look fertile so your grandchildren will need your help to understand how volcanoes add new minerals to the land and help us prosper. This is very evident by the two national monuments north and south of the Sunset Crater formation; when you visit them you need to remind the kids of the connection that these sites have with this seemingly desolate landscape.

The Lava Flow Trail is an easy walk that lets you examine the formations closely. If mobility is an issue, the first quarter-mile of the trail is totally accessible. The Sunset Crater Volcano is a cinder cone, the youngest variety of volcano. These form in a very short period of time, when a gas-charged froth of basalt explodes upward into a spray that cools before falling back to the ground. The volcano sometimes emits larger chunks (called volcanic bombs) too. Imagine a hailstorm where actual stones fall from the sky! As you drive through the Monument, the flow you will see happened after the gas was initially discharged, so this lava was not shot into the air.

At this monument it's easy to focus on the volcanic activity underfoot and ignore the massive peaks on the horizon—the San Francisco Mountains. They are also volcanic. Mt. Humphrey (12,633 feet), the highest mountain in Arizona, is part of this range. Like its neighbors, it is a volcano too.

Bonding and bridging:

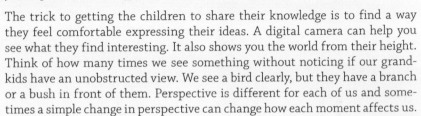

The monument staff provides a discovery pack that includes binoculars, a magnifying lens, a field journal, field guides and sketching materials. These are for loan, but it would be wise to check in advance that some are still available. In fact, you might want to make your own version of this pack for your grandchild so that they can bring it to all the parks and places you explore. For older grandchildren, add a digital camera.

The trick to getting the children to share their knowledge is to find a way they feel comfortable expressing their ideas. A digital camera can help you see what they find interesting. It also shows you the world from their height. Think of how many times we see something without noticing if our grandkids have an unobstructed view. We see a bird clearly, but they have a branch or a bush in front of them. Perspective is different for each of us and sometimes a simple change in perspective can change how each moment affects us.

A word to the wise:

Drive to the Snowbowl in the San Francisco Peaks. This ski area provides the best aerial view of the crater field whether from the parking lot or the ski lift. Sometimes it takes distance to gain enough perspective to understand the complexity of a geological landscape. Can you picture where the other two monuments are in connection with the Craters? (Hint: Bring a map and binoculars.) Drawing a map or taking photos is a good exercise in interpretation. If you check ahead of time, there may be a ranger to interpret what you see from this vantage point.

Age of grandchild: 8 and up

Best season: Spring–fall

Contact: Flagstaff Area National Monuments, 6400 N Hwy 89, Flagstaff, AZ 86004 • (928) 526-0502 • www.nps.gov/sucr

Geologic information: http://pubs.usgs.gov/fs/2001/fs017-01

Volcano sites in Arizona: http://vulcan.wr.usgs.gov/volcanoes/arizona/description_arizona_volcanoes.html

Also check out:

Walnut Canyon National Monument: www.nps.gov/waca

Meteor Crater

What is more exciting than an invasion from outer space? What is more compelling than the thought that our planet is going to be invaded by extraterrestrials? There is an entire genre of books and films based on this premise, but of course we tend to pooh-pooh the idea as nothing but fantasy. The dinosaurs might laugh at the idea, but of course they can't, as they were destroyed

when a space projectile crashed into the Yucatan peninsula. These "visitors from space" are meteors completing a cosmic journey, one that ends with a collision with earth—and a crater.

One collision created a crater that is more stunning than all the rest, and that crater is found in Arizona between Flagstaff and Winslow. It is the most unusual of all landforms in a state that is renowned for its landforms. This is a real crater made by an extraterrestrial impact.

Before you even arrive, spend an evening with binoculars and look at the moon. That brilliant hunk of rock is pockmarked with craters. Unlike the earth, the moon is not tectonically active, so evidence of impacts isn't usually quickly erased.

As you approach the crater, you are lulled by the predictable appearance of the landscape, yet suddenly the land rises and a ridge protrudes from the plains as you move towards the parking lot of the Crater Visitor Center. Enter the museum and you are surrounded by a modern astronomical story. Here you will learn about meteorites that have crashed through house roofs and into parked cars. You will see photos of fiery streaks flashing across the skies and early people cringing in fear or seeking enlightenment. Then you will learn about courageous and innovative scientists who managed to ascertain that meteorites and comets caused such craters. The size and scope of the impact that occurred here are almost beyond imagination. Take your time in the visitor center, then sit in the auditorium and watch the film that condenses the story and gives you a visual sense of what an impact would be like.

Once outside, you can follow a guide who provides lots of perspective and information, or you can go out by yourself and observe, photograph and speculate. Go with the guide only if your grandchild is old enough and interested and engaged. If they are, the crater is truly magnificent and captivating.

Bonding and bridging:

Here is a great chance to teach your grandchild about how science works. Take what you have learned at Meteor Crater and go to a beach or even a sandbox, then gather a variety of rocks of different weights and different sizes. What kind of crater do you get when you drop a rock that is heavy versus light; when it comes from an angle or straight down?

What happens if the rock hits water instead of sand? Some skip, then sink. Some sink straight down. Simple science like this won't provide many profound answers, but it is the way to begin some basic investigations.

At the Meteor Crater we can appreciate something exciting and unusual. This place helps us realize that the universe is so large and complex that no one person can understand everything there is to know. Even so, there is room for each of us to watch the skies and to learn about this amazing place we live in and its unusual stories.

A word to the wise:

Grandchildren may become concerned after learning about the devastation that occurs when a meteorite strikes, but the chance of experiencing such an impact in our lifetimes is miniscule. However, young grandchildren cannot always discern the difference between what is possible and what is probable, so you have to be the buffer. You want them to learn about this wild and woolly universe, but you don't want them to have night terrors. Help them by explaining that the meteor crater would not be so fascinating if there were millions of them. It is rarity that makes this site so special and we can take comfort in the fact that the meteor crater is 50,000 years old; in fact, it is older than any city or culture on earth. Let them know about the advances of science and if you go to Lowell Observatory or Kitt Peak you can let them see that people are actively watching the dark night sky and helping us to sleep easy.

Age of grandchild: 10 and up

Best season: Any

Contact: Meteor Crater Enterprises, Inc.: PO Box 30940, Flagstaff, AZ 86003-0940 • (928) 289-2362 • www.meteorcrater.com

Also check out:

Lowell Observatory, Flagstaff: www.lowell.edu

Life is no brief candle to me. It is a sort of splendid torch which I've got hold of for the moment and I want to make it burn as brightly as possible before handing it on to the future generations. George Bernard Shaw

Grand Canyon Railway

I have always loved riding trains, ever since my mom took my brother and me on a trip to Chicago when I was 8 years old. The sound of the wheels clacking on the rails, the rocking of the cars, as if on the ocean, made it an adventure of grand proportions, even though we were only traveling from Minneapolis.

Arizona has a very special train route, unlike any other in the US. This is a train that takes you to the very rim of our country's most famous and breathtaking

natural wonder. The Atchison, Topeka and Santa Fe Railroad began this service in 1901, mainly as a way to bring tourists to the Grand Canyon. There had been some thought that it would also carry ore from mining interests, but this proved unsustainable, while the tourist trade continued to grow, partly due to President Roosevelt's creation of the Grand Canyon National Monument in 1908. Business continued to boom until the 1960s when train travel quickly lost ground to the private car. As ridership fell, it looked as though the train was headed for the dust bin of history. It ceased operations in 1968. Luckily, in 1989 two people, Max Beigert and his wife Thelma, announced the redevelopment of the Grand Canyon Railway route. Because of their vision and passion for preserving a piece of Arizona history, we can once again ride the rails along this high desert landscape.

There is a sense of camaraderie on the train and you're allowed to move about and visit with other passengers. Kids often seem to find someone their age to chat with. Traveling at 45 mph, the scenery passing the windows is enjoyable and identifiable too. Occasionally prairie dogs, elk, mule deer, pronghorn and even mountain lions are seen. This is a very comfortable form of travel and grandparents probably have fond memories of trains.

Each car has a "conductor" who entertains and informs passengers about the history of the area and the train. Wandering cowboy musicians come through the cars and play a few tunes for your entertainment, and what Old West train trip would be complete without a group of train robbers riding up and stopping the train, so they can get on board and go through the car demanding money (and making everyone laugh). The trip takes two hours one-way and leaves early enough in the morning (and returns late enough in the afternoon) to give enough time to enjoy the great chasm and marvel at the beauty created over the eons.

Bonding and bridging:

There are a few other train trip options in the state, but whichever you choose, let your grandchildren help you plan the trip. Planning for a journey is half the fun and helps build anticipation. If you have a train set at home, set it up before or after the trip and relive the fun. If you rode the train across the US as a child, tell them how that felt. Talk about the ways travel has changed since you were young. Did your family have just one car? Ask them whether they think travel will be different in the future and whether they think trains should become a more important part of our transportation system. If you have the financial resources and time, it is great to spend a night in one of the park's hotels or cabins on the South Rim. This will give you more time to explore the amazing geology and take in some of the naturalist programs offered at the park. No matter what you choose, this will be an experience your grandchild will cherish.

A word to the wise:

This adventure costs money (in the ballpark of $100), but there are different levels of cost, depending on how much you are willing or able to spend. Basically you are limited to the Coach and First Class cars. (The Observation car does not allow children under 15 years old.) Both Coach and First class cars are restored from earlier eras of train travel and that is part of the fun. In the Coach car you will be sitting on bench seats and in First Class there are individual reclining seats. Both types of cars include the strolling musicians and entertaining "conductors," but first class also includes complementary snacks on both the morning and afternoon runs.

Age of grandchild: 5 and up

Best season: All year

Contact: 233 N Grand Canyon Boulevard, Williams, AZ 86046 • (800) 843-8724 • www.thetrain.com

Also check out:

Verde Canyon Railroad: www.verdecanyonrr.com • (800) 582-7245

I don't intentionally spoil my grandkids. It's just that correcting them often takes more energy than I have left. Gene Perret

Monument Valley

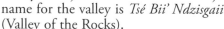

Imagine a place so inspiring that movies from the John Wayne classics *Stagecoach* and *She Wore a Yellow Ribbon* to *National Lampoon's Vacation* and Tom Hanks' *Forrest Gump* keep using the location as a natural backdrop in their storytelling. This is Monument Valley Navajo Tribal Park. The Navajo name for the valley is *Tsé Bii' Ndzisgaii* (Valley of the Rocks).

This is a place to visit during sunrise and sunset, when the angle of the sun is low. It is a place where you can ride hot air balloons in the chill of the early morning or travel by road during the morning or evening. You can enjoy the magnificent shadows that seem to move like they are endowed with the spirits of the land. It is also a place where you can hire Navajo guides to lead you in jeeps, on hikes or on horseback and experience the land and its history through the narration of someone intimately familiar with the scenery.

This landscape has been part of indigenous life dating back to the early people some call the Anasazi—the people who originally inhabited Mesa Verde and Canyon de Chelly. Over 100 archaeological sites have been identified so far. Far from being a remote land, it was a place where people lived their daily lives. It is good to talk about this as you explore the natural wonders. How would you be able to survive here? What would you eat, where would you live, how would you get water?

The road is very rough and even though it is only 17 miles, you should allow for a minimum of two hours, which should provide time for stops, photos and exploration. There is a hiking trail around the Mitten (a well-known formation) that is two hours long and could be hiked if you are prepared for sun and dry conditions. (The more ways you see a place, the better you get to know it.)

To add to the experience, you can consider these options as well: There are overnight rides in the park with guides, and a new hotel complex with amazing views of the rock formations is located at the visitor center and offers good food and places to visit. Just outside the park are stands where local Navajo Indians sell their crafts and artwork.

Bonding and bridging:

Take your time among these thousand-foot natural sculptures. With names like "the Mitten," "Gray Whiskers," "the Elephant" and "the Three Sisters," they should inspire children to see the magical qualities of the area. Tell them the names of some of the formations and challenge them to find the places that match the names. It might lead them to suggest names they would give the rocks and that can be a good place to share conversations and perspectives.

This is a national park, but it is part of the Navajo Nation. Do you and your grandchildren realize that the indigenous people of America still have the right to be independent nations and the Navajo have the largest part of their original lands of any of the Native nations? This is their place and they have set it aside in respect for nature and beauty.

A word to the wise:

Monument Valley Celebration Day in June includes the annual Drums of Summer and more family activities, which encourages visitors to engage in an entire day of music, dance, tribal traditional costumes, a trade show and even a fireworks display. Events like this bring Monument Valley to life and provide a context for the traditional cultures. The connection between people and the land has always been important, and seeing people in their own landscape is the best way to help your grandchildren understand this.

Age of grandchild: 8 and up

Best season: Avoid both the extreme heat of midsummer and the cold of midwinter

Contact: Monument Valley Navajo Tribal Park, PO Box 360289, Monument Valley, UT 84536 • (435) 727-5874 • www.navajonationparks. org/htm/monumentvalley.htm

Navajo Parks & Recreation Department, PO Box 2520, Window Rock, AZ 86515 • (928) 871-6647 • www.navajonationparks.org

Also check out:

Antelope Canyon, Page: www.navajonationparks.org/htm/antelopecanyon.htm

Through my grandmother's eyes, I can see more clearly the way things used to be, the way things ought to be, and most important of all, the way things really are. ED CUNNINGHAM

The World of the Diné (the Navajo)

It is refreshing to find an indigenous culture located where its ancestors dwelled, to be among the rocks and canyons where their stories and their spirits are at home. Northeast Arizona is such a place, and Tuba City is a good place to begin. Here, you'll find the Navajo Interactive Museum.

Originally designed and displayed for the Olympics in Utah, this museum in the Painted Desert tells the story of the "Navajo: People of the Fourth Dimension" and features exhibits, live demonstrations, films, and experts who take you around the hogan (a variety of Navajo house) that rests in the center of the display. You can easily explore Navajo oral traditions, the use of native plants, and traditional skills with your grandchildren. Take your time, listen and discuss, watch the basket weavers or wool spinners and examine the sand paintings.

When you are saturated with tradition and culture, walk outside to the Code Talkers Museum. The code talkers were Navajos and US Marines who fought in the Pacific Theater and developed a code based on the Navajo language that was used from Guadalcanal to Okinawa. There were 29 in 1942 and 550 by the end of the war. The code was never broken and was instrumental in the US victory.

From here you will want to go to Navajo National Monument. This is a land that is high in the pinyon and juniper woodlands with ancient communities like Betatakin and Keet Seel. Betatakin alone has 135 rooms and a kiva (a room for religious rituals) and the Ledge House, which is sheltered in an alcove 452 feet high. When you see this construction you will marvel at the creative strength of the people who lived in this demanding and difficult land. How did they select their sites? How did they construct these large structures without the tools we use today?

The Aspen and Sandal trails take you to these remote places, but they do include 300 feet of elevation change so you must judge your stamina, the heat and the terrain. The guided trip to Betatakin is 4 hours long and 5 miles roundtrip, which may be too difficult for some. If you decide to do the hike, arrive early (it is limited to 25 people on a first-come basis). Sunscreen, hats and lots of water and a few snacks are recommended.

Bonding and bridging:

Indian reservations are governed by tribal councils instead of the state or local government. Can you explain to the children how the Navajo and other native people were the first owners, the first occupants of this land we call America, yet they were restricted to lands that the United States declared reservations? What does the term mean? The nation reserved certain lands for the original inhabitants and took the other lands. Are these the places that the people want to be? Some, like the Navajo, are in their original homeland, while others like the Cherokee were forced to move far away.

There are so many things that you can talk about here. Big ideas can be introduced to the grandchildren, but do not be surprised if you run out of answers to their questions. If you don't have an answer, say so and suggest that you both try to learn more.

A word to the wise:

The Navajo are taught not to make direct eye contact, one of the little cultural differences you should teach your grandchildren about. It is always correct to learn the customs of the places that you visit, whether they are neighbors, or from abroad. Navajo are also taught not to be loud or talk too much and a strong handshake is not acceptable for this reserved culture that does not engage in touching. While they are constrained by the laws of the United States, Navajo still retain special rights and require non-Navajo to stay on the roads and pavement unless they are accompanied by a native guide.

Age of grandchild: 8 and up

Best season: May and September

Contact: Navajo Interactive Museum, Tuba City: (928) 283-5441

Navajo National Monument, 52 miles from Tuba City: (928) 672-2700 • www.nps.gov/nava

Also check out:

Hubbell Trading Post National Historic Site, Ganado: www.nps.gov/hutr

The Hopi Tribe: (928) 734-3100

Quechan Museum, Winter Haven: (760) 572-0661

Perfect love sometimes does not come until grandchildren are born. WELSH PROVERB

Canyon de Chelly

Canyon de Chelly is one of the most beautiful and exciting canyons in Arizona, a National Monument on the Navajo reservation that is both historic and contemporary.

There is a road that follows the two branches of the canyon, the "Y" that brings the two ancient streams together, and it is filled with inspirational overviews and stops that allow you to look down into the majestic canyon,

but it does not really provide the satisfaction you will want. It is a sampler, not a full experience. For you to truly experience this land requires an indigenous guide; this is an opportunity, not an imposition. By jeep or by horseback you can travel the sandy bottom of the canyon and experience the cliffs as the ancient people did, rising to the sky, bold patterns of rock against a blue sky. Here you can wander among the cottonwoods and discover the unique communities of kivas and houses, see the footholds carved in the sandstone, and observe pictures painted on rock by individuals a thousand years ago.

You can arrange the guide through the visitor center or one of the area motels and then you have the advantage of both access to the inner canyon and also the knowledge and companionship of a person who lives within the Canyon for at least part of the year. This exciting aspect exposes visitors to historical and contemporary Indian society, and is a reminder that in a land that seems to have a short history, the real story of the people and the land actually dates back thousands, if not tens of thousands, of years.

Today this land is a national park that belongs to another nation—the Navajo—and as you travel it is important to visit with your guides and learn about life in this region.

As you look at these communities you can talk about how people lived and whether our small rural towns are different from these historic locations. You will get off the horse or jeep at times and you can touch the sandstone, look up at the canyon tops and examine the structures and ask yourself how you would have survived in such a place.

Bonding and bridging:

The pictographs here are so vivid they look like they are recent, but many of the animals drawn on the walls no long reside in the region and most of the time the riverbed is a wide ribbon of sand. There are trees that have been planted in the valley and you should talk about what happened to the original vegetation and why the trees were put in place. Did the ancient people have more water or less? What are the reasons? The museums you visit and the visitor center at the Park entrance can help you to understand and investigate these questions.

The basic pictograph is a simple illustration but has great meaning. Ask your grandchildren to make a pictograph that shows something they find important. Do this each day of the trip and keep their pictographs as you would photographs in your album. Let them develop patterns, choose colors and explain what message they want to give those who look at their creations.

A word to the wise:

We are used to snapping photographs of anything and anyone we see. This is inappropriate and insulting to many Native people throughout the world and if you want to take a photo of someone (including your guides), ask first. Talk to them about what is appropriate and how to handle requests. They are willing to work with you to make a good experience. Talk to your grandchildren about this beforehand, how they would feel if people suddenly came into their neighborhood and took photographs of them no matter what they were doing and wanted to photograph their friends and family, their rooms and their toys. What would they do if they did not want someone to take their picture? This is an excellent start to respect for cultures and one another.

Age of grandchild: 10 and up

Best season: Spring and fall

Contact: PO Box 588, Chinle, AZ 86503 • www.nps.gov/cach

Also check out:

Navajo National Monument, Kayenta: www.nps.gov/nava

Wupatki National Monument, Flagstaff: www.nps.gov/wupa

Walnut Canyon National Monument, Flagstaff: www.nps.gov/waca

It's funny what happens when you become a grandparent. You start to act all goofy and do things you never thought you'd do. It's terrific. MIKE KRZYZEWSKI

They Call It Grand

In our society we have a propensity for hyperbole. If someone is good at something we say they are a superstar, if they give maximum effort we say they gave 110%. So here we are with a place called the Grand Canyon and all we can say is that the name is an understatement. But what else could you call it? Super Canyon seems cheap, Really Big Canyon sounds like something you'd find in Lake Wobegon. So we say this is a place for Grand Parents with Grand Kids to experience the truly GRAND!!!

Exploring the south rim of the Grand Canyon is easier than the north rim. Even on the south rim, the trails skirt close to the edge, which can trigger one's fear of heights and falling. These are places you want to avoid with young children, but as your grandchild gets older, these dramatic points are important for finding perspective.

Free shuttle buses traveling the roads allow you to walk from overlook to overlook and make the trail as long or short as you desire. The buses come regularly within short intervals making the logistics of a rim walk easy and pleasant.

Getting to the north rim is much more difficult, and it is located at a higher elevation. The north rim is a destination for older grandchildren who enjoy a more wilderness experience. They can walk in higher elevation pine and spruce on the north, while the south rim is yucca and pinyon pine.

On the south side there are many locations with shelters with refreshments and souvenirs. Avoid these if you want the hike to just be an adventure, but if you want to have a breather, then the south rim offers the easier options.

If you're planning on venturing down into the canyon, it's easier to do so on the south rim because of the lower elevation. The north rim is 2,000 feet higher in elevation, and at that altitude, the air is less oxygen rich. Burro rides can save you from the suffering that climbing and high elevation can bring, so consider them an option. If you feel that your feet are a better way to have a true experience, just remember that your hike up will feel like twice the length, so walk down one hour and expect at least two hours to cover the same ground going up.

Bonding and bridging:

How do you share the Canyon? No one can take it in with the first look. Photographs are good and everyone on the trip should take them, not just one person. Painting and drawing are also good and if you choose art, take the time needed to make art. If you rush the experience your grandchild will not experience the pace and perspective of nature that is so much a part of a place like this. To hurry, to rush in and out of the bus is not a way to share. Take time and give time to look at the birds soaring in and above the canyon (the California Condor is here). Watch the elk graze and the sun work through the shadows. If there is anything more valuable than the gift of a sense of time and place, we have not discovered it.

Also keep in mind that an experience like this should not consist of going from souvenir shop to souvenir shop. A cheap gift does not represent a one-of-a-kind experience.

A word to the wise:

No one enjoys being completely out of breath, which means you should consider carefully which rim of the canyon you plan to visit, and whether you're going to venture down into the canyon. This means you have to consider how comfortable you are with the grandchildren walking on paths near sheer dropoffs, too. The great aspect of this canyon is that you can experience it without handrails and fences, but that is also the great drawback, because it means you have to also be extra cautious for yourself and your grandchild. When done right and when you stay within your limits, this experience can be with you both forever.

Age of grandchild: 8 and up (kids younger can have a good experience, but there are a lot of worries)

Best season: Late spring and fall

Contact: Grand Canyon National Park: PO Box 129, Grand Canyon, AZ 86023 • (928) 638-7888 • www.nps.gov/grca

Also check out:

Skywalk and Hualapai Reservation: www.destinationgrandcanyon.com

Kaibab National Forest: www.fs.fed.us/r3/kai/

Family faces are magic mirrors. Looking at people who belong to us, we see the past, present and future. GAIL LUMET BUCKLEY

Lake Havasu:
The Big Lake of Arizona

In a state where lakes are really reservoirs and the image that the rest of the world has is desert and saguaros, you might be as fascinated as we are about boats and boat owners in Arizona.

You may hear people in Arizona say they have more boat registrations per capita than any other state, but this is a bit of an exaggeration, since the state comes in 43rd. Still, you might be surprised at just how many boats you do see in a state with so many deserts. There are numerous small lakes around the state, but the real boating places are Lake Havasu, Glen Canyon and Lake Powell. These massive waters are unique given the contrast between them and the arid landscapes. They are beautiful and striking regardless of how you feel about the dams themselves. There are many boating options in each of these places, some very expensive, some very simple. It is an activity where grandparents who have a relationship with both water and watercraft can share their connection, something that seems to be quite easy since children seem to take to water with very little encouragement.

Lake Havasu City was planned and created in 1963. This makes it a very young city and one that grew up around the water, and it includes one very unique feature—the London Bridge—a massive, historic landmark that was moved stone by stone from England. For the children, it is the childhood rhyme come to life, only they'll see that the London Bridge is quite sturdy and not likely to fall down! You can rent boats of all descriptions below the bridge and you can go sightseeing, fishing and exploring. It is cool, refreshing and fun. The pontoon boats are especially fun for them since there is more movement allowed on these floating platforms. If you prefer not to get on the water, there are a variety of state parks along the river and along the channel where you can swim or play on beaches. Lake Powell is known for houseboating, an activity that is relaxing but also expensive, so be prepared if this is the watery adventure you are looking for. Being on a houseboat is something few children ever experience. The houseboat allows for longer trips and more exploration, but if you are adventurous or experienced and have older grandchildren, guided sea kayak trips can take you into the drowned canyons and give you access to remote landscapes.

Bonding and bridging:

There are many ways to enjoy the National Recreation Area including bicycling and hiking. While the water captures our attention, the recreation area also encompasses wonderful wild landscapes for those who are fit and wanting to explore by land. Both Glen Canyon and Lake Mead National Recreation Areas have bike trails and many campgrounds so that you can enjoy these locations even if you don't own or rent a boat.

The recreation areas also have visitor centers where you can participate in ranger activities and your grandchildren can take part in junior naturalist programs. To highlight contrasts in nature, lead them on one of the short desert hikes and compare what grows near the water with the arid rock landscape away from it. Let them know that this is not a natural landscape and while beautiful we still have to be wise when altering any landscape this much.

A word to the wise:

These lakes can be really crowded and the whine of the personal watercrafts can be annoying. The waters can be rough from winds, but also from the convergence of so many wakes and this sometimes causes seasickness. These are not reasons to stay home, but realities you need to be prepared for. Needless to say, a houseboat requires that you are comfortable with the water and that you take extra precautions for the children's safety. Insist that younger grandchildren wear a life jacket at all times.

Age of grandchild: All

Best season: May–September

Contact: Lake Havasu State Park: 699 London Bridge Road, Lake Havasu, AZ 86403 • (928) 855-2784 • http://azstateparks.com/parks/laha

Glen Canyon National Recreation Area: PO Box 1507, Page, AZ 86040 • (928) 608-6200 • www.nps.gov/glca

Lake Mead National Recreation Area: 601 Nevada Way, Boulder City, NV 89005 • (702) 293-8906 • www.nps.gov/lake

Cattail Cove State Park: PO Box 1990, Lake Havasu City, AZ 86405 • (928) 855-1223 • http://azstateparks.com/parks/caco

Also check out:

Lake Havasu: www.golakehavasu.com.

Oasis in the Desert

Yuma is set in the middle of the Mojave Desert, but the Colorado River runs along the edge of town and creates a linear oasis. This oasis has palm trees, but it also has mesquite, palo verde, cottonwoods and a green parkway connected by walking and bike trails.

The Spanish, who came to this area in the 1500s, noticed that there was a natural crossing of the Colorado River here. Fort Yuma became the first settlement and between the 1850s and 1870s a town was established and the river was the source of life and transportation. Steamboats transported people and materials to various mines and military outposts and the town grew, moving away from the river.

Two historic state parks document the time when Yuma was a rough-and-tumble town on the frontier. The Quartermaster Depot State Park has a number of restored buildings that contain historical artifacts and exhibits related to the depot's use as a supply station for troops in the Arizona territory in the late 1800s. Just across the railroad tracks is the Yuma Territorial Prison State Historic Park. While landscaped beautifully with flowering shrubs and green grass, it still reminds us of the harsh life both prisoners and guards endured. One can still smell the dankness coming from the thick-walled adobe buildings. A cemetery just down the hill holds the remains of 100 prisoners, but all that marks the graves are piles of stones.

The bike path is paved and follows the river, where West Wetland Park is a sharp contrast to the prison. There is a disc (Frisbee) course for the older kids, and for the younger ones there is the most impressive Stewart Vincent Wolfe Memorial Creative Playground, built by community members in 10 days. Designed like a castle with a maze of steps and hallways and slides built into it, kids can spend hours just running in, around and out of it. A path that acts as a "moat" circles the castle and has a number of very well designed signs that focus on trees and plants and their importance in our lives. These will be better viewed once the kids have exhausted themselves on the playground equipment. Across from the playground is a quiet Hummingbird garden with paths that meander among the trees and signage that tells you more about these special birds. During the wet season, the wetlands are visible down below and are home to many more species of birds.

Bonding and bridging:

Yuma came into existence because of the presence of water. In this case it was the mighty Colorado River. Without that source of life-giving liquid none of the subsequent development would have occurred. A visit to an oasis, like this one, gives grandparents a great opportunity to talk about water and its importance in our lives, no matter where we live, but this is especially true in a desert region. People of all ages are becoming more conscious of our use of this natural resource and the critical need to protect and conserve it. If you have always lived in Arizona you can talk about the difference in peoples' attitudes about water when you were young and what they are now. If you come from another, more water-rich state, you can share your perspective on living with and without an abundance of it. Let the kids tell you how they think we can best conserve water.

A word to the wise:

If you walk down from the Prison State Park towards the cemetery, stay to the paved paths as much as possible, as the non-paved paths are loose gravel and rock and too easy to slip on—not just for the grandparents but for rambunctious youngsters too. There is a small beach at the river at the Crossings Park, and some people may choose to swim there, but there is no lifeguard on duty. Also, if you'd like to use one of the many ramadas for a family picnic, you must call in advance for a reservation.

Age of grandchild: Toddler to teenager

Best season: Fall through spring

Contact: Yuma Territorial Prison State Historic Park: 1 Prison Hill Road, Yuma, AZ 85364 • (928) 783-4771 • www.pr.state.az.us/parks/YUTE

Yuma Quartermaster Depot State Historic Park: 201 N. 4th Avenue, Yuma, AZ 85364 • (928) 783-0071 • www.pr.state.az.us/parks/YUQU

Yuma Crossing Heritage Area: 180 W First Street, Suite E, Yuma, AZ 85364 • (928) 373-5198 • www.yumaheritage.com; visit www. AZStateParks.com or call (928) 373-5243 to reserve a picnic ramada in Gateway Park

Also check out:

Encanto Park, Phoenix: www.visitphoenix.com

Pow Wow

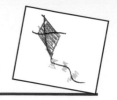

No one knows how pow wows began, although there are many theories. The word "pow wow" is believed to be from the Narragansett Tribe and refers to a curing ceremony. Some think that pow wows were started by the war dances of the Ponca.

Now, imagine a warm sunny day, at Pioneer Park in Mesa, with a Mormon Temple on one side of the street and drums beating a rhythm among bleachers, tents and palm trees on the other. You hear singing, a cadence that is repetitious and in sync with the drum. The voices are singing words in another language and for most of us, a language of another time. There are people of all ages; some wear feathers and headdresses, beads and bells. These are representatives of American Indian nations from all over the continent.

There is no charge and you can come and go, wander the grounds, and observe. On Friday there is a concert and Saturday and Sunday there are dances which go on all afternoon, but we recommend you be there for the "Gourd Dance" and the "Grand Entry." Seeing these two dances allows your grandchildren to observe that in all cultures, dance has many forms.

The Gourd Dance precedes the Grand Entry. It is said to come from the Kiowa and Comanche, but its origins are a little vague. Gourd Dancers wear a long-sleeved shirt and pants with a gourd sash or vest and carry a tin or silver "gourd" filled with beads that they shake as they move their heels to the sound of the drum. Then at the correct moment the groups or sets of dancers move away from one another.

The Grand Entry is done in the sacred circle, which represents the circle of life. Veterans, elders, princesses and organizers are honored. The Indian anthem is played and the sense of inclusion takes in the audience as well. The rules of the pow wow are simple—no drugs, no profanity, no cutting across the dance circle and ask before taking photographs of anyone.

Your grandchildren will feel the drumbeat and might want to move to the rhythm too. Let them. It is important for them to sense the history in this event and watch the intense concentration of the dancers who are caught in the music and the story that the dance represents.

Bonding and bridging:

The United States is known as the "melting pot" for good reason. Our country consists of diverse groups, varying cultures and many different backgrounds. A pow wow is an excellent chance to expose your grandchildren to the traditions of the indigenous peoples of America.

Ask your grandchildren what they think about their identity. (This is a tough concept, so help them with a few examples, but don't give them the answer you want to hear, let them tell you who they think they are.) Ask what traditions they and their family celebrate; this will help them to understand what traditions are. What are the special days and events that mark their year? It is also a good time to remind them that like the people at the pow wow, we should celebrate all those who came before us, those who have sacrificed for us, and all the life that surrounds us.

A word to the wise:

In the midst of this energy and color there are many things that you can learn—among them respect for other beliefs and ideas. Either before or after the pow wow it would be good to visit the Heard Museum in Phoenix, the Arizona Museum on the Campus in Tucson, the Navajo Interactive Museum in Tuba City or the Navajo Nation Museum in Window Rock. This will put native cultures in perspective and it will also make the museums more exciting and relevant.

Age of grandchild: All

Best season: Fall, winter, spring

Contact: The Roy Track Memorial Pow Wow: City of Mesa Parks and Recreation Department, 480-644-2352

Also check out:

Annual Hoop Dance Contest, Heard Museum, Phoenix: www.heard.org/hoop

Apache Gold Casino Pow Wow: www.apachegoldcasinoresort.com

Arizona State Pow Wow, Tempe: http://powwow.asu.edu

Native American Month Social Pow Wow, Tucson: www.usaindianinfo.org

They say genes skip generations. Maybe that's why grandparents find their grandchildren so likeable. Joan McIntosh

Rodeo

Is there a stronger image of the Old West than the cowboy on a bucking bronc? The American West has long been more myth than reality, but the cowboy is the one true image that continues to survive because he does not need exaggeration; he is the working man and the relationship he has with his

horse, the cattle and the range make for exceptional images. All of these images come together in the rodeo.

You can choose a variety of locations to explore the rodeo circuit. The La Fiesta de Los Vaqueros Rodeo takes place during the 3rd week in February in Tucson, and it also features kids events like sheep riding (the children are wrapped in protective gear and covered with a helmet for this bucking contest). There is also a Junior Rodeo so your grandchildren can see contestants from 5–12 years old competing in a variety of events. The Mike Cervi Jr. Memorial Team Roping event is an outstanding exhibit and contest that features amazing lasso skills!

According to the Rodeo Hall of Fame, "the only real "American Sport" began July 4, 1869, when a group of bragging cowboys took their skills into a bronc riding contest, with the winner getting a new suit of clothes." This became the professional sport when businessmen in Prescott organized the first "cowboy tournament" in 1888. The term rodeo was not used until 1916 and was not adopted for the Prescott contest until 1924. Today the rodeo is part of Frontier Days, so celebrations abound inside and outside the rodeo arena.

In early September you can find the Pine Country Rodeo in Flagstaff or attend the Chino Valley Territorial Rodeo, but for something really different you can go to the all-Indian rodeo on Labor Day in Window Rock. It combines traditional song and dance, Indian Crafts, fireworks, concerts and a celebration of youth. Chinle also offers an all-Indian rodeo at the Navajo Fair in combination with a pow wow and festivities. This is a chance to let the grandchildren see that American Indians were renowned for their horse-riding skills.

A good rodeo requires that both athletes—the rider and the horse—be in great shape, and at a rodeo you'll see a contest where care is given to both. The rodeo clowns play an important role too; while they dress funny and act goofy, their job is to do their best to protect the cowboy and the horse.

Bonding and bridging:

For many of our grandchildren, life on the range, the ranch and life on the horse is lost. Westerns are no longer the common fare on television and in the theater, and many children live in cities where horses are only seen in parades and petting zoos, but not part of everyday life. But people who have worked with animals have a special understanding of the animal's strength and personality, and all have richer lives because of this relationship.

How did we learn to live and work with animals? Can you research this together? And when you do, check out the rodeo events and see what parts of ranch life each event represents.

A word to the wise:

Talk to your grandchildren about animals. For the older grandchild or one who is especially concerned about animal welfare, rodeos can raise a lot of questions. Some people consider them cruel. Should animals be used in this way to entertain us? You may be surprised by the opinions of your grandchild on this topic.

Age of grandchild: 7 and up

Best season: February–September

Contact: La Fiesta de Los Vaqueros, Tucson: www.tucsonrodeo.com

Also check out:

Desert Thunder Pro Rodeo, Tucson: www.desertthunder.com

World's Oldest Rodeo, Prescott: www.worldsoldestrodeo.com

Pine Country Rodeo, Flagstaff: www.pinecountryprorodeo.com

Navajo Nation Fair Rodeo, Chinle: www.navajonationfair.com.

Snowflake Rodeo, Pioneer Days, Snowflake: www.snowflaketaylorchamber.org

Listing of rodeos: www.arizona-leisure.com/arizona-rodeos.html

The simplest toy, one which even the youngest child can operate, is called a grandparent. Sam Levenson

Baseball All Year

While the Diamondbacks represent Arizona during major league baseball's regular season and the postseason, and all professional and college sports can provide great experiences for grandparents and grandchildren, it is major league baseball's spring training that provides the experience we most recommend. The teams are

all in Phoenix or Tucson so the chances of finding a game near you are always good—just go to the stadium closest to you or watch your favorite team.

Spring training in the Cactus League is a glorious time when athletes shrug winter off their shoulders and everyone is fresh and anxious to pick up a bat and a glove again. The games don't count, except for those young and old players who are fighting for a roster spot. Fans can enjoy the games of catch, batting practice and the infield drills, and these can be as much fun as the exhibitions. A little game of catch with your grandchild before and after the game will cement the experience and add to the day.

In the fall league, there are fewer teams and they only play in the Phoenix area. Fall league is for prospects, that is, for young players who hope to become major leaguers. Usually the team consists of players from 4 or 5 teams and the atmosphere is even more relaxed than spring training, so there is no real team to root for. The crowds are tiny and the price of admission is cheap.

This is a time to concentrate on the game and its history. Watch how the pitcher winds up, how the catcher frames a landing place for the ball. Where are the infielders and outfielders? Do they change locations? Why? Like chess, it is all about moving the pieces, but unlike chess, this game has human variables and that makes each game special. Watch them warm up and see the smiles and laughs. This is good to point out because in the end, this is a game, and games should be fun.

The fall league is truly an introduction to professional baseball, while spring training is a celebration of the new season and a rite of spring. It is about new hope and possibility, while the fall league teaches us that no matter who just won the World Series, life goes on. If you can teach your grandchild sportsmanship, ethics and a positive outlook, then the game will have been the framework for a wonderful gift.

Bonding and bridging:

The fall and spring leagues are places to relax and enjoy the beauty of the game. Here you can learn about players as people, you can tell stories about the past and players you rooted for when you were young. Hot dogs, popcorn and soft drinks are less expensive than in the regular season and the sun is warm and relaxing.

Foul balls are easier to catch at this time of year and a baseball glove is a handy accessory. It is also good to learn ballpark manners. Yes, you can yell and cheer, but you talk about poor sportsmanship and poor behavior. Teach them to be a good person in everything that they do. If you ask for autographs remember that the players are people like you and it is good to use the player's name and say "please" and "thank you." You should also have a Sharpie pen and something for them to sign. They will appreciate it and it will make a better experience for all of you.

A word to the wise:

Autographs are better in the spring and fall than during regular season. The players are more relaxed and they like to sign for the kids. This is not about getting some valuable autograph to be sold, it is your grandchild and a good experience that will be remembered. The first row of the stands adjacent to the home bullpen is often a good place as well as the rows by the clubhouse entrance. The back ballfields may have many future stars in a relaxed atmosphere and you might get the signature of a future Hall of Famer giving your grandchildren a reason to root for them.

Age of grandchild: 6 and up

Best season: Spring and fall

Contact: Arizona Fall League: http://mlb.mlb.com/mlb/events/winter-leagues/league.jsp?league=afl

Also check out:

Spring training planner: www.cactusleague.com

Glendale Stadium-Camelback Ranch: www.arizona-vacation-planner.com/glendale-stadium.html

Goodyear Ballpark: www.arizona-vacation-planner.com/goodyear-ballpark.html

Everyone needs to have access both to grandparents and grandchildren in order to be a full human being. MARGARET MEAD

Bike Arizona

What a state! Climb, hike, drive, ride the train, fly, glide, balloon, ski and bike. The options are amazing and bicycling is one of those sports that quickly brings generations together. However, you need to be careful and take your grandchildren on a trail, not roads. On a bike trail there is exercise and fresh air for both of you, great scenery and a sense of accomplishment, all of which are essential elements to making a wonderful day.

The history of this simple contraption is somewhat lost in the mists of time, but drawings and prototypes go back to the year 1400 or so (yes it is older than us grandparents). The first one was like a scooter, but it was soon improved

on (1818) by a German, Karl von Drais de Sauerbrun. It had two wheels and a handlebar, but one thing was missing, the pedals! After that, the Velocipede was invented, but it made for a pretty uncomfortable ride (it was referred to as the "boneshaker"). The next version of the bicycle after the Velocipede had a large front wheel and was called the "high-bicycle" or the "penny-farthing." It wasn't until the 1880s that the "safety bicycle"—what we'd refer to as the bike today—was invented and became popular. AARP reflects on the value of biking for grandparents: "Bicycling gives you a low-impact, aerobic workout that strengthens your legs, including your knees. It also can help you lose pounds and stay a healthy weight." For children, biking is a way to connect them to the outdoors, to give them valuable aerobic exercise, as well as a tool to prevent obesity and to help them feel a sense of accomplishment.

Fortunately we have many bike trails to choose from that are safely removed from cars and other hazards. Like choosing whether to canoe or go hiking, you must consider your fitness, the weather and the terrain. The terrain might even be the most important factor to consider—hills make for difficult biking and if you are not in shape, they are frustrating. Check out Arizona's state parks and the area's national parks. Many communities (Flagstaff, Yuma, Tucson, Mesa, Tempe and Reid Park in Tucson) also feature paved bike trails away from vehicular traffic. In addition, the Rails to Trails organization lists numerous options like Apache Railroad Multi-Use Trail and Indian Springs Trail in Apache County, Peavine Trail in Yavapai County and Route 66 Trail in Coconino County.

Bonding and bridging:

When biking, your ambition needs to match the skill and endurance of your grandchildren. Keep in mind that you are doing this with—and for—them and make accommodations if you need to pedal more or less than they do. Making the right choice isn't difficult—take a short ride with younger children and a longer ride with older ones.

Pack a lunch, bring a camera, stop and reflect and relax. A trail is an adventure if approached in the right way and not just a connection between beginning and end. Make it interesting and share your love of a silent sport, the satisfaction of using your own physical power to move, and a speed that allows you to observe and enjoy.

Keep track of your rides in a biking journal. Miles, altitude and favorite memories should all be recorded. Someday, they might return with their own grandchildren.

A word to the wise:

There are some wonderful options for taking young children on a bike ride. Kate has an old-fashioned trailer that fastens to the seat stem and serves as a carriage for the child. Newer, more lightweight models are available today. Attachable seats that are very similar to car seats are also available. They fasten to the handlebars and frame and the child is between your arms and facing forward as you peddle. A third option is a bike attachment that adds an extra wheel and seat behind your bike. This is like creating a tandem bike, but is designed for smaller peddlers. Just like an overloaded car, when you're traveling with a young child, you will coast faster and your brakes will have to work harder. You might not slow down as fast as you want. An accident is the last thing you want, so use extra caution, not extra speed. And finally, remember that there will be extra work involved for you, so keep stamina in mind.

Age of grandchild: 3 and up with child carriers, 10 and up for extended rides

Best season: Spring, fall and winter

Contact: Flagstaff biking: http://flagstaffbiking.org/

Also check out:

Arizona bike tours: www.azbikeped.org/bicycle-touring-and-recreation.html

At age seven, children have as passionate a longing for creative interactions and learning as they earlier had for explorations of the world. Joseph Chilton Pearce, *The Magical Child*

Bird Watching

In the world of birdwatching, Arizona stands out as one of the premier places to see rare and unusual species. While we have arbitrary borders with fences to designate what is our land and what isn't, birds don't. They fly where they have always flown, based on the seasons and habitat needs. In the spring many species fly north from the tropics, some going all the way to the tundra. But there are some beautiful species that only fly as far north as Arizona. Because of this annual influx, the state lists 531 species, nearly double what many northern states list. Just listen to the names: Elegant trogon, elf owl, red-faced warbler, painted redstart, sulphur-bellied flycatcher . . . and you know that it is a treasure trove of feathered beauties.

No single activity between people and nature has as many participants as bird watching. Nothing captures our love of nature, love of flying, the beauty of wild animals, and the sense of the hunt, the way bird watching does. Some will argue with our statement about hunting, but that is only when we limit our definition of the hunt to killing, rather than finding.

Grandchildren love to play hide and seek, they enjoy the challenge of trying to solve riddles, they like fast action, and they love animals. Combine those elements into an activity that grandparents can enjoy and participate in, and you have a recipe for fun.

Arizona has a magnificent variety of ecological zones, from deserts to mountains to meadows, and each one provides different food and habitat for animals. Mammals tend to come out at night, reptiles stay hidden and amphibians only call for a short time and then are hard to find. But birds are active, colorful, sing, and can be seen in the air, and in the trees and on the ground.

The Southeastern Arizona Birding Trail is an effort to map out the bird life of this portion of the state and provide you with hints on where to birdwatch. A special map helps you follow the trail; it is a treasure map of a different sort. It lists over 50 sites, including state parks, wildlife refuges, recreation areas and conservation areas and some private property, along with descriptions of habitat, location and best seasons to visit. The maps can help you plot a weekend-long (or longer) birding expedition, with locations identified by numbers on the roads.

Bonding and bridging:

The best place to begin birdwatching with your grandchildren is right at home. All you need are one or more
birdfeeders situated so you can see them from your
windows. Be sure to have at least one hummingbird
feeder, since they are both beautiful and entertaining
to watch. You can begin with a grandchild of any age,
but the younger the better. Try to identify a few species
and then when you go on walks or visit other locations, point
out the birds you see together.

Birding festivals are another option to help your grandchild develop this
shared hobby. They can be found around the state from January through
August (check the Watchable Wildlife website for dates and locations). Here
you will learn from the experts and participate in a variety of bird-related
activities and talks. Birdwatching groups are always excited to see youngsters
being introduced to this "sport" and will share their knowledge willingly.

A word to the wise:

If you are beginning with young children, get a pair of toy binoculars so that
they can become accustomed to putting them up to their eyes and finding
the birds—these toys do not really magnify, but they teach a skill that can be
difficult even for adults to learn. When they graduate to real binoculars, you
can practice on fence posts and various still objects. Turn and focus. Be sure
the eyepieces are set to the right width for the grandchild and show them how
to focus. To make it easy, when you begin, have them always put the focus
wheel all the way to one side so they always have to move it in one direction
only. Make everything as easy and foolproof as possible.

Age of grandchild: 7 and up

Best season: Spring and summer

Contact: Southeastern Arizona Birding Trail: www.seazbirdingtrail.com

Audubon Arizona: http://az.audubon.org

Tucson Audubon Society: (520) 629-0510 • www.tucsonaudubon.org

Arizona Watchable Wildlife Tourism Assoc.: www.azwatchablewildlife.org

Also check out:

Bird watching for kids: www.birdwatching.com/tips/kids_birding.html

*Our children grow up so fast. Maybe grandchildren are God's way of
giving us a second chance at participating in the miracle of life.* Unknown

Grandparents Day

Ranking far below Mother's Day and Father's Day, this national holiday was established in 1973 in West Virginia through the efforts of Marian McQuade, a mother of 15 who was as dedicated to the care of senior citizens as she was to children. In her efforts to reach out to the generation of grandparents of her time, she formed the Forget-me-not Ambassadors to make sure that senior homes were visited regularly. In 1978, President Jimmy Carter recognized this effort and ushered in a national day of commemoration.

The day did not get instant recognition, but there is hope that those of us in the Baby Boomer generation will demand that this day be as venerated as the other days that honor parenting in all its forms.

It falls on the first Sunday after Labor Day, a day sure to be overlooked since it comes right after the last big holiday of summer, at the beginning of school, and in the transition to the school year, autumn and family schedules. But don't allow it to be forgotten. Instead, make it a day that brings your grandchildren in to honor the grandparent's life. Your children can help make this happen, but it can be a success if you do the planning too.

Board games still intrigue our grandchildren; the same with jigsaw puzzles, creating albums together, going for a walk, watching the bird feeder, telling stories. These things all work and sometimes your old idea will seem like a brand new and exciting discovery. Keep it simple.

Watch old movies or old TV shows that you watched when you were a child. Look at old photo albums (for a little while—don't overdo it). Sit and eat together; too many kids don't have family meals anymore, and set the table to be a little fancier to introduce them to special events.

The parents can help by providing the time. They can make sure that they bring the child over without additional stresses, and then they can leave and let the day be yours.

Bonding and bridging:

This day is not for going somewhere, not for outside entertainment, but it is good to go outside. The Baby Boomers are the last generation to have had a childhood without computers, VCRs, DVDs, CDs, color television. We grew up with empty lots and knew how to play with cardboard boxes. Consider a meal on the lawn, raking and playing in the leaves, playing croquet, or a little badminton.

If you have saved any old clothing—a little dress up can go a long ways too. Or pop some popcorn and gather around the old radio—if you were from the generation of radio drama. You can now order them on tape or CD. Turn off all but one lamp, sit on the floor and pull the easy chairs around the CD player. Have popcorn and lemonade and tune into the old radio experience. Because we have put so much stimuli in to our world, it takes a little effort to reduce the distractions and concentrate on the audio experience.

A word to the wise:

The smells of bread baking, flowers in our mothers' gardens, the tart crab apples in August, the sound of radio, all are part of our life experience. But nothing is more nostalgic than the candy we ate as children. We have had a wonderful time getting boxes of old time candy to share. Kids say, "What is that?" and our contemporaries say, "I remember eating that . . . " In fact, Mike's memories include the third drawer down on the right side of his grandfather's desk as the place where the bonbons were kept. They were the special treat shared with his grandfather during visits.

Age of grandchild: All ages

Best season: First Sunday after Labor Day

Contact: Your place or your children's home

Also check out:

For old time candy, try www.oldtimecandy.com or www.hometownfavorites.com and see if one of them might have the assortment that brings back memories to your tastebuds and shares a bit of your childhood with your grandchildren. We were flooded with nostalgia when we opened our first box and gave away numerous boxes to friends for Valentine's Day for the fun of sharing memories. Remember Mother's Day and Father's Day too!

*One way to open your eyes is to ask yourself,
'What if I had never seen this before? What if
I knew I would never see it again?''* RACHEL CARSON

Celebrating The Weather

Arizona is famous for the heat of the desert and the low humidity, but it is also a landscape of summer monsoons, snowy mountaintops, and dust storms. The mix of weather that is part of every year is dramatic and sometimes overwhelming, but it is also a chance to explore nature no matter where you are.

Grandparents can help grandchildren avoid weather phobia, which many children can develop if they spend too much time watching the Weather Channel, where the emphasis is often on severe weather. This can be harder in the city when the only interaction with nature is getting to the car, the office, the school, etc. Then it is a nuisance, but should it be? Does it help to complain about the weather? (Of course we're not referring to tornadoes and other dangerous storms, nor does it refer to the changes that our own careless pollution and disregard might cause to the climate.)

Think back to your childhood. Did you always want to come in when it rained? Did you want to be inside because it was cold or snowy? We know our grandsons would like to be out playing and if that is not possible they still want a fun day. So here is the challenge to all grandparents: Figure out and set aside some special activities for the most challenging weather.

Getting dirty is normal and not something to avoid. Do you remember running out in the rain, jumping in puddles, making mud pies? Many of these things don't happen as often now. Not because the kids wouldn't enjoy them, but because it is easier to bring them inside. Small children think an umbrella is fun and they need to walk with you in the rain. Children in Arizona don't often get a chance to see snow, but if you take a trip north to the Flagstaff area in the winter months, be sure to bring a piece of black felt on a board, let it get cold, then catch snowflakes that you can look at with a magnifying glass. Their intricate designs and unique formations will fascinate both young and old. For most of the year, bad weather is caused by two things—the wrong clothes and the wrong attitude. You can help change that. Give your grandchildren the gift of that many more good days in their lives.

Bonding and bridging:

Everyone talks about the weather and unfortunately almost everyone complains about it. But what is weather, and how can they learn about it with you? Make a little weather station at your home and another to take with you. Then set up a journal for weather records. Wherever you are record the temperature in the shade and in the sun, if you can get a little handheld wind meter you can record the amount of wind and the direction (use a compass). A rain gauge is a good tool too and you should have a barometer, an indoor-outdoor thermometer and a humidity meter.

You can get small solar collectors and charge batteries of power toys or fans. The old-fashioned whirligigs that spin in the wind and kites are all weather machines. You can watch waves on a lake or sailboats on the water as well. The purchase of a simple digital weather station means they can have temperature, heat, humidity and rainfall all right where they can take notes.

A word to the wise:

We do not want to belittle weather. It is important to dress correctly and we need to know about sunscreen, windbreakers, rain jackets and warm clothing for cold conditions. And we need to make them aware that rainstorms can include lightning. But a child who has experienced weather in all its variety is one who is better prepared for its challenges. Weather has only four ingredients—wind, temperature, atmospheric pressure, and moisture—but think of how much variety those four elements can create!

Age of grandchild: 5 and up

Best season: All

Contact: Arizona weather from NOAA: www.weather.gov/view/states.php?state=az&map=on

Also check out:

Grand Canyon weather: www.grand.canyon.national-park.com/weather.htm

Arizona State Climate Office: www.public.asu.edu/~aunjs/azscclimate.html

Highway conditions: www.highwayconditions.com/az.htm

Arizona weather: arizonaweather.org

Weather for kids: www.weatherwizkids.com

Getting to know the youngest people in my life has been a joy. Frank Tarloff

Classic and Antique Car Shows

We are a car nation (and we're not talking about the flower). Mr. Ford did more than make it possible for every family to have a Model T, he set our nation on a path that would create a frenzy and love affair like nothing else in history. It might have been a rich man's toy to begin with, and the working man's transportation for later generations, but ultimately cars became an expression of who we are. I'm not what you call a "car guy," but I still love to see the automobiles of my generation. My father was a mechanic. He loved motors and the sound of his ratchet set clanking under the hood, but he couldn't pass his passion on to me. Instead, his granddaughter forsook her dolls for toy trucks and cars.

The automobiles of each generation reflect the society and the values of that time. Ford's Model T was a symbol of progress and innovation. In the 1950s the Thunderbird represented status and pride. Today we have trucks, minivans, and even Smart Cars!

A good car show features both vintage automobiles and some classic modifications, like the hot rods we saw at the first annual car and airplane show held in Mesa at the Commemorative Air Force Aviation Museum. Arizona has a climate that minimizes rust and allows the ancient wheels to shine proudly in the sun.

These vintage displays are all over the state, but the experience is about more than the cars. It's about memories and dreams. I find myself drawn to the 1949 Plymouths because that was my first car and represents a lot of memories. At the same time, I'm also drawn to others like the muscle cars of the 1950s with fins running wild. The cars will have hoods up and motors gleaming, the colors will be vivid and the shine will dazzle you in the Arizona sun. You can walk with your grandchild and see what gleams in their eyes while you talk about the wheels of your youth. Lead your grandchild around and share your stories, but let the child tell you which cars they like most. They will see color and shape in a way that is completely different from your memory-biased viewpoint. If there is a parade of cars you can enjoy the sound and sight of the past coming alive, but even if they simply sit on the blacktop, you can walk among friends and give your grandchildren a connection to the open road and your own past.

Bonding and bridging:

Cars have always been special. Driving your first car is a rite of passage, a sign of adulthood, and your grandchildren are well aware of this. Yet our infatuation with cars is about something even greater. Cars become part of our identities. For teenagers, the car is a symbol of independence and freedom. They are the open road, the wind at our back and the call of the horizon. For many of us the first car was what was available and affordable, often far from what we wished. But that didn't matter.

For your grandchild, a car symbolizes a longing to be an adult and a desire to create a personal identity. It is about growing up and you can explore that dream as you see what their favorite cars at the show are. You can learn about their color preferences and see if they share your love of line and airflow. After going to a car show, consider putting together a car model, another hobby from the past. Let the kids choose the model you will build.

A word to the wise:

If you choose the show at the Commemorative Air Force Aviation Museum you can combine a look at airplanes with the cars and see how the same technology was adapted to each use. In addition, the museum is an active flight museum and you can arrange to take a flight on a vintage airplane. Other car shows are part of celebrations and festivals. They come in a variety of locations and are all created for the car enthusiast to show off their vehicle. All types of collecting is personal so make the most of the owners' enthusiasm. Give them a chance to brag and share their love.

Age of grandchild: 5 and up

Best season: Not summer

Contact: CAF Aviation Museum: www.azcaf.org

Route 66 Car Club of Flagstaff: www.route66carclub.com

Flagstaff Route 66 Days: www.flagstaffroute66days.com

Also check out:

Hot Rod Planet: www.hotrodplanet.com

Now that I've reached the age where I need my children more than they need me, I really understand how grand it is to be a grandmother. MRS. MARGARET WHITLAM

Cooking with Your Grandchildren

Food comes from the grocery store! A little too simple, but a common belief among a large portion of urban children who do not see farms regularly, who do not hunt, fish or even cook! As grandparents, we have the opportunity to turn the kitchen into a science center. All types of cooking require reading recipes, math (measuring) and science (the interaction of compounds). So jump in, set aside the time, and start your grandchild on a new path.

Cooking with your grandchildren can add memories of all sorts, in a very positive way. Depending upon their age you can let them use a cookie cutter and decorate your creations, or they can participate in measuring, mixing, baking, and of course, eating.

Be prepared to do the majority of work. If they get bored and wander off, don't force them back. They will come back for the tasting. Be patient and let them get intrigued.

Success comes from following some simple rules: Choose a recipe your grandchild will like. This should be a very simple recipe to begin with, but in one case, we chose complex and challenging recipes to teach a teenager who really wanted to learn. She was motivated by the challenge.

Start by washing hands. Good hygiene is an important lesson and cleanliness might be tough to achieve, but keep it in mind. Put an apron on everyone and if you can find a chef's hat that fits them, the kids will feel even more grown up. Then, set out the ingredients. When you invite them to cook with you, the last thing you want to do is make them wait while you sort out your cupboards. Set up three "stations" that keep the children away from sharp knives and hot pans. One is for mixing ingredients, the second is the oven or stove for cooking, and the third is the spot for decorating or serving the results. Use a stool if necessary, so they can reach the counter. Help them measure, but do it over a separate bowl so that extra ingredients do not fall into your final product. As you work you can talk about the ingredients, where they come from, the difference between healthy and unhealthy food, and why we care about what we eat. For younger children, decorating is the most fun, although they enjoy eating quite a bit too. In fact, dough may start disappearing before it gets to the oven. How can you beat an activity that is tactile, has great scents, looks good, and tastes delicious?

Bonding and bridging:

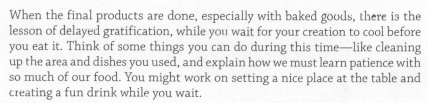

In our research we came upon a very significant state-ment: build kids, not cookies. What a great perspec-tive. This is all about sharing and creating. They are learning where food comes from, they are doing something that has a great outcome, and they are beginners. Do not even think of doing this unless you are able to invest the time. Don't rush, make sure to turn off the TV, and don't talk on the phone. This is not a time for multi-tasking, but a time for concentration.

When the final products are done, especially with baked goods, there is the lesson of delayed gratification, while you wait for your creation to cool before you eat it. Think of some things you can do during this time—like cleaning up the area and dishes you used, and explain how we must learn patience with so much of our food. You might work on setting a nice place at the table and creating a fun drink while you wait.

A word to the wise:

A good beginning exercise for young kids is making playdough. All you need is 7–8 cups of flour, 3 cups of salt, 3 tablespoons of cream of tartar, ¼ cup of vegetable oil, 4 cups of hot water, and some food coloring. Mix the first three, add oil and water and knead. Break up the dough into smaller units so you can make different colors when you knead. There are many things to do in a kitchen and depending on the age, you can parcel out the work. Two-year-olds can scrub and tear, three-year-olds can mix and pour, and four- and five-year-olds can learn to measure and beat. Once grandkids can read, the possibilities expand and soon they will be able to plan and make a full meal.

Age of grandchild: 3 and up

Best season: Any

Contact: Les Petites Gourmettes Children's Cooking School, Scottsdale: www.lespetitesgourmettes.com

Simply Impressive Cooking School, Mesa: www.simplyimpressivecooking.com

Also check out:

The science of cooking: www.exploratorium.edu/cooking

Joy in looking and comprehending is nature's most beautiful gift. ALBERT EINSTEIN

Ethnic Festivals

If you are like us, traveling with your grandchildren to visit all world's great cultures is beyond your financial means; however, participating in the ethnic festivals that dot the state is a way to explore the world. At these festivals everyone speaks English, dollars are the currency, yet the festivals help your grandchildren feel like they have taken a trip to a foreign land.

The Tucson Celtic Festival, like so many ethnic festivals, has a wide variety of activities for the grandchildren. The sound and sight of bagpipes is unique and fun, and what child won't be surprised by the sight of men wearing skirts? Be prepared for questions. Each culture has developed specific costumes and dance that relate to their past. Grandchildren can really relate to these performances because the majority of dancers are young. The Flagstaff Celtic Festival features an oatmeal toss (which must be seen to be believed) and an archaeological dig for children. In Phoenix, the Irish Fest provides an autumn variation on this theme with dancing, music and children's costume contests.

The annual Matsuri in Phoenix is a festival celebrating Japanese culture that includes *nihon buyo*, a classical dance, and the powerful, popular taiko drumming. Martial arts such as Shotokan Karate and Japanese fencing (Kendo) are also included. The Chinese Festival in Phoenix every February has unique food, arts and crafts, dragon dances, mah-jong contests and martial arts.

Chandler's Cinco de Mayo Festival and Chihuahua Race will really get kids excited. These miniscule doggies may not be greyhounds, but they have the spirit that is needed for a fun contest and include a king and queen Chihuahua. Fiesta de Septiembre in Wickenburg celebrates Mexican Independence Day with music, arts, food, mariachis, dance, and a kids zone where they can make salsa and other creations.

One of the most surprising events might be the Hawaiian and Polynesian Festival in Tempe. Called the Aloha Event, Tempe is transformed into a South Seas paradise with Tahitian drummers, slack guitars, hulas, fire dances, that combine to make this is a dynamic experience. You can also see outrigger canoes and listen to stories, some even accompanied by ukuleles!

Bonding and bridging:

Take a trip to adventure and exotic locations without an airline ticket! Learn about cultures, music and dance, observe strange sports, and eat wonderful food. What other enticements do you need to expand your grandchild's image of the world?

You can choose a festival that focuses on your own ethnic background and investigate your own heritage. Regardless of which festivals you choose, take photos for an album. With all the materials that are now available for scrapbooking, you can create a memory book that will feature the country, the sights, and as many of the sounds and tastes you can record. You can buy some cards and small items to add to the book as well. But the value will be in the discussion you have with your grandchild about the variety of people, cultures, languages, foods, and festivals that make the world so special and the need to respect the variety.

A word to the wise:

Your grandchild might be wise about geography, but most Americans aren't. Get a globe and locate the countries you visit at each festival. Add a flat map on the wall and mark it with your weekend travels. This kind of knowledge will serve your grandchildren well in school and is an incentive-filled method for understanding geography and culture.

Age of grandchild: All

Best season: All seasons

Contact: Tucson Celtic Festival, Tucson: http://tucsoncelticfestival.org

Arizona Highland Celtic Festival, Flagstaff: (928) 556-3161 • www.nachs.info/festival.shtml

Arizona Matsuri: Phoenix, AZ 85069 • http://azmatsuri.org

Cinco de Mayo Celebration & Chihuahua Races: www.chandleraz.gov/default.aspx?pageid=161

Also check out:

Phoenix Chinese Week: http://phoenixchineseweek.org

The Aloha Event: http://www.azalohafest.org

Farmers Markets

Maybe you've had the good fortune to travel to Europe and wander through the colorful, lively and fascinating outdoor markets. Almost every town or village has one day in the week when farmers come to town to sell their produce. It is a social occasion as well, where friends and neighbors meet and chat, and children chase one another around the legs of the adults.

I was lucky to have a grandmother who had been a farmer and when she moved to the city, a weekly trip to the farmers market was her way to keep that part of her past alive. As a child there were many Saturday mornings when I was roused from my bed at dawn to accompany my mother and grandmother to the market. Any grumpiness I felt at this intrusion on my weekend was erased as soon as I smelled the ripe cantaloupe (or musk-melons as my grandmother called them). The memories of those Saturday mornings with her among the multicolored and sensuous smells of the earth's bounty are some of the best I have.

Arizona is blessed with a climate that allows crops to grow nearly year-round; the limiting factor is water, and as such you will find different products at these farmers markets than you would out east or in the midwest. Roasted peppers, bottled salsa, homemade mesquite tortillas, prickly pear jelly; these are just some of the specialties to be found, in addition to more familiar vegetables and lots of other jellies and jams.

In today's world very few children have the experience of caring for animals, picking food for the evening meal, or even running free in the pasture. A farmers market, with its colorful tables of produce, flowers, meats and baked goods may be as close as many children will get to being at a farm, or meeting a farmer.

There are so many lessons in this visit. Think about all of the contrasts between a farmers market and supermarket, such as the packaging (or lack thereof). Also consider what healthy food is and what the word "organic" means. Above all, go early and wander leisurely. Some markets may have music, sometimes there are samples to nibble, and there is always great people watching. The smells, sounds, textures and colors are images that will stay with your grandchild—just as these images have stayed with me.

Bonding and bridging:

It's easy to take food for granted. Whenever we want it, we know where to get it. A simple trip to the grocery store takes care of our needs. Rarely do we consider the question, "Where does this food come from?"

A farmers market is a chance to open your grandchild's eyes to the hard work and dedication that go into everything we eat. Tell your grandchild how important farmers are to our way of life. Share how difficult it is to grow crops and how we would struggle if there were no farmers. Either way, this is definitely a time when you want to help your grandchild learn to appreciate their every meal. Ask your grandchild to think about what they'd like to have for lunch or dinner, and then make the goal of your visit to find the best ingredients—it can become a treasure hunt. Even the pickiest eater probably likes tomatoes, corn on the cob or watermelon. To complete the morning's excursion, let him choose a bouquet of freshly cut flowers to put on the table.

A word to the wise:

Another option, besides farmers markets, is to take a ride into the country and visit a farm that sells its produce directly to the customer. Some of these farms, especially fruit orchards, are "Pick Your Own" establishments, so you make this a shared experience. The best selections are available from July through October. One site to check is www.willcoxchamber.com and look at "visiting the community." This will get you to a link with a listing of direct-sale farms, and the food they sell.

Age of grandchild: Toddlers through teenagers

Best season: Midsummer through October

Contact: www.arizonafarmersmarkets.com

Also check out:

www.foodconnect.org/farmers_markets/index.asp

www.azda.gov/cdp/farmersinfo.htm

There is no other door to knowledge than the door Nature opens. And there is no truth but the truth we discover in Nature. LUTHER BURBANK

125

Geocaching

Arizona is a state that is famous for its treasures, both lost and found. In a land where people still dream of buried treasures, geocaching represents the excitement of the hunt in search of a "treasure," albeit not a lot of riches.

When geocaching, your task is to enter the coordinates of a cache on your GPS (the cache is the treasure that someone has hidden and challenged you to find), and then let the GPS guide you to it. A GPS unit is a handheld instrument that allows you to do difficult things easily. GPS systems can tell you where you are, how to get where you want to go, even showing you the path you've already traveled. It can tell you height and distance, travel speed, and even the time you rested. They do all this by communicating with satellites. (Of course, all technology has it limits. When it cannot find satellites, it cannot find you. When there are too few satellites, its accuracy is compromised.) In short, a GPS system serves as your travel guide, as it includes a feature that allows you to return to your home, car, or starting point. (Yes, you do have to learn how to use your device, but it really is not that hard!)

Once you're in the general vicinity of the cache you must use your wits to find it. When you locate it, open it up, sign the little guestbook, and if you take a treasure, you will be expected to leave a replacement (this is more about sharing than taking). Then when you get home you can upload your photos and your success on the website.

More importantly, geocaching is an independent way of finding your way through the forest, desert, wilderness and city parks. There are literally thousands of geocaching sites all over the world and more than 5,000 in Arizona, so begin with the geocaching website and register your family with international and state groups. Then begin with places nearby or places where you are comfortable. Your grandchildren will love being part of this excitement so make sure that they get to do everything, but there is a warning: this can be addictive.

Now state parks and forests have joined and most public land has something to discover, just be safe and enjoy the scenery while you hunt. There are even geocaches in the zoos, parks, and places that you have been visiting for years; now you can return and discover these old friends from a new perspective.

Bonding and bridging:

The GPS only knows how to point straight at the destination; it does not understand that cliffs, lakes, rivers and other obstacles exist. Using a map, reading the terrain, determining time and distance allow you to make good and safe choices. Talk about the decisions to be made. Who should you let know about your activity in case something goes wrong? What should you tell them? What food and drink should you bring? How about a first aid kit? Should you have a shelter in case something goes wrong? Do you intend to split your group up? Will a cell phone work in that area? What can you bring for the next person who finds the cache?

And finally, if you really enjoy this activity, think of how much fun it would be to create your own geocache! You can plan what to put in it and where to hide it, then you can register it and begin to invite people from all over the world to follow your tracks.

A word to the wise:

While it is easy to get excited about the GPS unit and the way that it can work in our car and in our hand, it is important to teach basic navigation skills too, especially how to use a map and compass. The GPS unit is wonderful, but what if the clouds are too thick, the forest too dense, the rocks too close or the batteries too old? When we rely on batteries we limit the time we can be confident, but when we know how to use a compass to find direction and we know how to use a map to plan a route and find our way through the landscape, we have basic life skills that can be used anywhere and anytime. The compass is a simple instrument and it can be taught easily. Aligning it with a map is more difficult. Practice and prepare ahead of time. Use a map when driving and then use a map when walking and let your grandchild see how to determine where they are and how to find their way back to the beginning.

Age of grandchild: 6 and up

Best season: All year, but not in the heat

Contact: Arizona Geocaching: www.azgeocaching.com

Also check out:

International geocaching website: www.geocaching.com

Take a Lake Break

In a state where water all seems to be stored in cactus or found in the water traps on a golf course, it is a luxury to find a place to swim that is not a pool, and the state park system provides some access to the rare waters of Arizona. Children are naturally drawn to water and a place like Roper State Park is irresistible. The water is not just cooling, but magic. For young children, if a sand beach is nearby, the magic continues, as they can shape these two seemingly commonplace things into sandcastles and roads.

Unlike Roper, Lake Havasu State Park gives access to the popular reservoir lake that has become a vacation hotspot. Here you have cold, clear water to play in and if you have a boat, you can enjoy sports like waterskiing and fishing. Like all lake environments, this is good for birds and provides trees in the midst of the Mojave desert, perfect for shady picnics.

If your grandchild has caught the fishing bug, you can take them for the hard-fighting bass at Alamo State Park (near Lake Havasu in the Bill Williams River Valley) and then enjoy the clear skies and the constellations. For many children, the concept of watching the sky without telescopes is something new, as it is something many cannot do in their urban backyards. Maybe you can even watch the skies as they are reflected in the lake, or watch the sparkling embers of your campfire dance in the darkness like miniature meteors that fizzle quickly.

Fool Hollow Lake Recreation Area combines fishing and cold, refreshing mountain air and lets you enjoy 100-foot-tall mountain pines. Motor sizes on Fool's Hollow Lake are restricted, so quiet is the order of the day. And if you want to fish for trout, you and your grandchild can find them at Patagonia Lake State Park where they are stocked every three weeks from October–April.

The ingredients are there and the options are located all around the state. Giant waterways at Page on Lake Powell, at Lake Mead and at Lake Havasu have resorts, boat ramps and, often, houseboat rentals.

The decision on what to do is up to you, your health, your personal interests, and your resources. A walk along a shaded lake is easy and free, a picnic and skipping rocks costs only the price of the items on the menu, but the value of the shared experience will last a lifetime.

Bonding and bridging:

Fishing is about much more than catching. True anglers enjoy the environment and the challenge of knowing the fish that they are after. It is good to start kids with bluegills and crappies, to hook them with easy success, but eventually you will want to teach them the finer points of fishing. Why do people practice catch-and-release? What is the value of letting the large fish go back to breed?

What is life like under the water? If there is a naturalist program at the park, you can join them to help explore this question. As you fish, you can watch the birds, see the insects, and discover more species that depend upon the lake. Join naturalists to look at dragonflies and damselflies, inform children that fly-fishermen use their knowledge of the lives and movements of various aquatic insects for their sport.

A word to the wise:

At places like Roper Lake State Park there is competition for space on the water, as there is only a small amount of water compared to a very large demand. Here the region's water crisis can be seen in miniature. Arizona is gaining people and losing water that cannot be replenished. Streams that once received rain almost year-round are now dry. This is a good place to talk about conservation and our finite natural resources.

Age of grandchild: All

Best season: All year for lake experiences, check the laws for fishing

Contact: Alamo Lake State Park: PO Box 38, Wenden, AZ 85357 • (928) 669-2088 • http://azstateparks.com/parks/alla

Patagonia Lake State Park: 400 Patagonia Lake Road, Patagonia, AZ 85624 • (520) 287-6965 • http://azstateparks.com/Parks/pala

Fool Hollow Lake Recreation Area, 1500 N Fool Hollow Lake Road, Show Low, AZ 85901 • (928) 537-3680 • http://azstateparks.com/parks/foho

Roper Lake State Park 101 E Roper Lake Road, Safford, AZ 85547 • (928) 428-6760 • www.pr.state.az.us/parks/rola

Also check out:

Lake Havasu State Park: 699 London Bridge Road, Lake Havasu, AZ 86403 • (928) 855-2784 • http://azstateparks.com/parks/laha

Sunshine is delicious, rain is refreshing, wind braces us up, snow is exhilarating; there's really no such thing as bad weather, only different kinds of good weather. John Ruskin

Tea Parties

Among the most powerful childhood memories I have of my mother is an event she called "Having a tea party with Mrs. McGillicuddy." I have no idea who Mrs. McGillicuddy was or how she came up with that name, but it succeeded in setting the tone for an afternoon of fun. I can't remember much else, except my absolute, sheer delight and amazement that my mom could act so silly and playful.

Unfortunately, in our culture, tea parties have a gender bias and are associated with girls. (In contrast, men and women alike enjoy tea breaks and even something called high tea in the British Isles.) It may be difficult to sell a grandson on the idea of a tea party, but that's not to say you shouldn't try. Almost all kids love dressing up and play acting, taking on the role of someone else, especially if that someone else is an adult character.

There are several options for these tea parties. First the child may host a party for a collection of their favorite stuffed animals or dolls; second, they may host a party for a small group of friends; or third, adults such as parents and/or grandparents can serve as the participants. You can help facilitate the first two, but to have the most fun, the third option is the best choice.

A good tea party involves dressing up in some old formalwear, sitting around a little table and drinking tea (or make-believe tea). Set the table with your good dishes or a set of child-sized plates and cups. Add a flower centerpiece, and maybe even make invitations. Maybe you want to choose new names for the party—something old fashioned and formal. Adopt an accent. Ham it up. Hold your cup with your pinky raised up. Find some funny, fancy clothes or hats to wear and then get ready for the fun to begin.

For more realism, make little sandwiches and desserts—the grandchild can help with these preparations. Mix a variety of teas (those with a sweeter flavor are probably best), but have other beverages such as lemonade or juice available.

Your grandchild will be amazed that you can act like someone else, and they will be tickled by your willingness to play this "game" with them. Giggles and laughter will erupt frequently—guaranteed.

Bonding and bridging:

One of the nicer aspects of a tea party is the occasion to slow down and live in the moment. All of our lives seem to be on fast forward these days. Tea time is leisurely and relaxed, even as we seek to teach manners. For all the play involved, there are lessons to be shared. In our society, civility and manners are disappearing. Use your time together to demonstrate old-fashioned table etiquette, with the use of the silverware and polite conversation. (Make sure your cell phone is turned off too.) These are skills that can be used in so many situations as the grandchild grows older. You can also recount for them what you remember about your first restaurant visit. Going "out to eat" is such a common occurrence in families today, they may be shocked to learn that when you were a child, going to a restaurant was usually a special occasion.

A word to the wise:

Read the section in *Alice In Wonderland* where the Mad Hatter hosts a tea party. This may inspire future parties, as well as introduce the child to some classic literature. The important point is to keep the entire event fun, so that they want to do this again. As the child matures and demonstrates an ability to enjoy this kind of semi-formal setting, you can reward them with a visit to a real Tea Room or High Tea. There are many options listed on the websites below.

Age of grandchild: 5 and older

Best season: Anytime

Contact: Tea time traditions: www.seedsofknowledge.com/whimsy.html

Also check out:

Arizona tearooms: www.teamap.com/states/state_AZ_Name.html

Cemetery Visit

We know that this sounds a little morbid in the midst of all the adventures and discoveries that we recommend, but sometimes there are stories that need to be told and sometimes grandparents are the best teachers.

You might visit a cemetery where a loved one is buried and begin a personal journey to find your past and your grandchild's heritage. Seeing your family name on a tombstone raises questions about who is buried there, and why. In other instances the cemetery transcends family and personal connections. That is how the "boothill graveyard" of Tombstone feels. We can see the Jewish and Chinese sections, but mostly we see that over 300 bodies are buried here and few are identified. In fact, the Jewish cemetery was lost for years until a Yaqui Indian helped to restore it. Boothill's original markers were mostly stolen for souvenirs, a callous act that disregarded any respect for history and the individuals. As you look at the markers you might talk about why people would do this?

Sometimes the cemetery is the story, like the burial grounds at Yuma Territorial Prison where the piles of rocks delineate the last place on earth for prisoners who left little behind to mark their passage. In all, 111 prisoners died here and only 7 were claimed by their families.

Then there are cemeteries like the one in Wickenburg where the headstones seem to create a tableau that speaks of both the lost and the survivors. These are strong stories that tell about our bonds with one another and death's inevitability. Near San Xavier del Bac Mission the graveyard is large and represents the mix of Native and Latino populations that came to the Mission.

What will you do at the cemetery? You can see the symbols that people find important, you can talk about how difficult it is to let someone you love go from your life and what we do to keep them part of ourselves? You can talk about famines and wars, and the diseases that claimed the young before we had the inoculations to stop the spread of terrible epidemics. This is the reality of the cemetery, but while we are alive we have the chance to make life beautiful and productive. We owe it to those who were here before to make the world as wonderful as we can and to celebrate the lives of our ancestors.

Bonding and bridging:

Death is obviously represented in each tombstone and marker, and of course, each grandparent must recognize that if life goes as it should, we will be the first loved one that our grandchildren will mourn. But you need not be morbid about the fact. You need not even bring it up. Eventually they will, just as one of our grandchildren did after his dog died. Death is cruel and we know no easy way to deal with it, but each person seeks some solace or path, whether by religion, or by intellect.

In the cemetery you can let your child explore and see the symbols of hope, the words and their message. Visit the oldest markers to acknowledge the pioneers and to establish the fact that history is made of all people and not just the famous. Above all, make it okay to visit the cemetery, all right to talk about life and death, and let your grandchild set the tone and ask the questions. These are not spooky places, but places of honor and remembrance.

A word to the wise:

We tend to associate ghosts with cemeteries, so maybe it is natural to make visits to ghost towns a part of this story. Ghost towns are part of the Arizona landscape, places where hopes soared, disappointments rose, and efforts were abandoned. Are these monuments to dreams any different than cemeteries? When you visit one of these old towns or see a building aging in the fields, ask your grandchild about the people who lived in those towns. Talk about the people who were in the cemetery and the various ways we leave a part of us behind.

Age of grandchild: 8 and up

Best season: Any

Contact: Historic AZ cemeteries: www.azhistcemeteries.org/azcems.htm

Also check out:

Boot Hill Cemetery, Tombstone:
www.interment.net/data/us/az/cochise/boothill/boothill.htm

Yuma Territorial Prison Cemetery:
www.interment.net/data/us/az/yuma/prison/prison.htm

Library

Did you know that libraries are not an American invention or a creation of Mr. Carnegie? The Sumerians had a "House of Tablets." Imagine what it would have been like when everything was written on a clay tablet? The ancient Egyptians were the first to create a "House of Books" and they are credited with coming up with the form that would be the standard for books for the

rest of civilization, even though books themselves changed over time. A major development in books and the creation of libraries came much later. Your grandchildren should know about Andrew Carnegie, because he built 2,509 libraries between 1881 and 1917, mostly in America, the British Isles and Canada. Open to the public, libraries have been one of the greatest successes for freedom of speech in the world. Finding these old giants is like finding parts of the history of libraries; make it one of your challenges.

All libraries are wonderful and offer great opportunities and treasures, but some also combine the excitement of an historic structure which means the library is a story in and of itself. Look up a book that you think would be fun and then help the child find it. If you have any trouble, ask a librarian to help. Somewhat like geocaching, the children learn to follow instructions and get a reward for their success.

The Children's Museum in Tucson is located in an old Carnegie library which seems like a nice shift of usage for this building since it was dedicated to increased knowledge and insight. The Carnegie Center in Phoenix is now home to the Library Development Division of Arizona State Library. Can you find other old giants and discover their stories? Or perhaps you would prefer a very modern and spacious library like the new Prescott Valley Library.

Many libraries have a special section for children that are colorful and often have small imaginative structures within them along with stuffed animals, and, of course, appropriate books. It is good to go into one of these sections and sit and read a book with your grandchild. To give the grandchild a special library experience, you can start by helping them apply for their own library card. This is an amazing possession because it gives them access to all the great books in the building. Let them understand that they can take books home and then return them to acquire more. The process of checking out a book is exciting and caring for a book and returning it teaches responsibility.

Bonding and bridging:

Even in the age of computers, books are still a repository of knowledge and feelings. They are intimate capsules of knowledge that can be touched, held, investigated. You can still see that intimacy with your young grandchildren who are excited by the story time that libraries offer.

A fundamental goal of libraries is to instill in people (especially children) a lifelong love of reading and provide learning opportunities through books and various media types. Visiting a library together can foster a special relationship between the generations by bonding over the magic of a shared book. Perhaps the highlight of a grandchild's visit is that calm period of reading at home just before bed. It is a time when the book is a magical bridge between you and the grandchild, between wakefulness and sleep and between generations and across imaginations.

A word to the wise:

Most libraries offer story time when the librarians read selected books. The readers use great voices and sounds, incorporate music and often movement to interact with the children, and the book becomes a magical device to connect everyone. Enabling this to happen is great, but it is important that you are there with them. By being attentive and participating, you show them that this wonderful experience is something you value too.

Age of grandchild: All

Best season: Any season, but the summer is a great time to avoid the heat

Contact: A reference to all state libraries: www.librarysites.info/states/az.htm

Also check out:

Arizona Public Libraries: www.publiclibraries.com/arizona.htm

Arizona Historical Society: www.arizonahistoricalsociety.org

Carnegie Center, Phoenix: www.lib.az.us/carnegie/history.cfm

Chino Valley Children's Library: www.chinoaz.net/library/childrens.shtml

Phoenix Public Library children's page: www.phoenixpubliclibrary.org/kids/default.jsp?N=7105

Index

About the Authors

Mike Link:

Mike Link is the author of 22 books and numerous magazine articles. He and his wife Kate live in Willow River, Minnesota, where they enjoy having their grandchildren discover the world of nature and play. The bird feeders are always full and the forest has wonderful trails.

For 37 years Mike directed the Audubon Center and now, entering retirement, he is looking forward to writing, teaching for both Northland College and Hamline University, and of course spending time with the grandchildren.

As his books attest, traveling is another passion. With fifty states and twenty countries covering his travels, paddles, hikes, and explorations, he feels that he owes a debt to the earth. Whether we call it Mother Nature, Gaia or Creation, the earth is our source of air, water and sustenance and its destruction is a crime.

Their son Jon has continued to carry the family outdoor tradition into the wilds of Alaska as a kayak ranger with his wife Kristin. Daughter Julie is raising grandson Matthew. Mike's son Matt died in a kayak accident in New Zealand and little Matthew is a spirited tribute to his uncle. Alyssa has her hands full with twins Aren and Ryan and little Annalise.

Kate Crowley:

Since marrying Mike and moving to the country twenty-two years ago, she has been surrounded by forests, prairies, birds, dogs, cats, horses and lots of other wild creatures.

When Mike built her Lady Slipper Cottage in the woods, her dream expanded, but it wasn't complete until she became a grandmother.

Kate has been a naturalist, an educator, and a writer for 30 years, first at the Minnesota Zoo and then the Audubon Center of the North Woods. She has co-authored 12 books with Mike and writes for magazines and a monthly nature newspaper column. Kate enjoys hiking, biking, skiing, scrapbooking, reading and spending as much time as possible with her grandchildren. She cares deeply about preserving the natural world.

Visit Mike and Kate's website at www.GrandparentsAmericanStyle.com